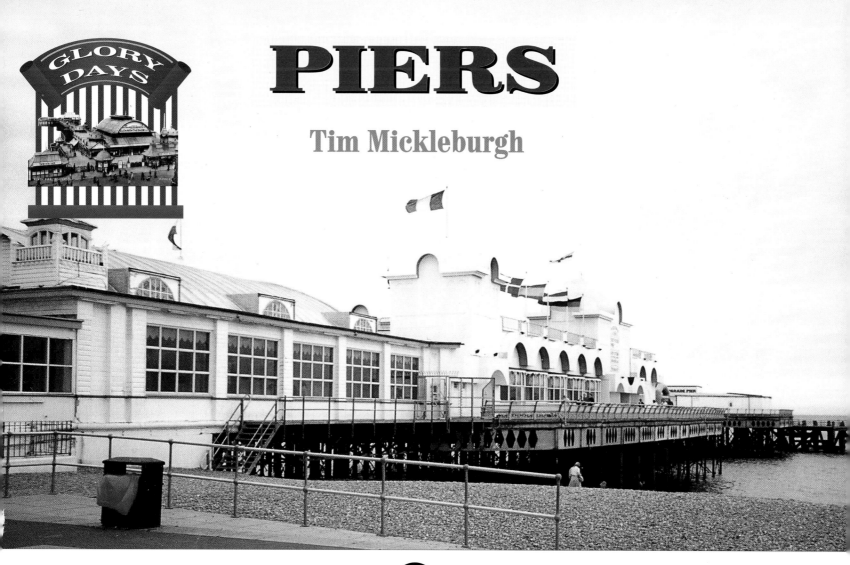

PIERS

Tim Mickleburgh

DIAL HOUSE

Title page:
SOUTHSEA, SOUTH PARADE – Not quite as grand as before, the seaward end pavilion houses showbars and amusements. It is visible to thousands crossing by the Isle of Wight ferry from adjacent Portsmouth.
Andrew Monro Collection

Front cover:
CROMER – A 500ft iron pier replaced a second jetty, and opened in 1901. The bandstand was extended in 1905 to form a pavilion, and this can clearly be seen in this pre-World War 1 view.
John Haddaway collection

Back cover:
SOUTHAMPTON ROYAL PIER – c1910, showing a train in the station.
Author's Collection

CONTENTS

First published 1999

ISBN 0 7110 2655 6

Published by Dial House

an imprint of Ian Allan Publishing Ltd, Terminal House, Shepperton, Surrey TW17 8AS.
Printed by Ian Allan Printing Ltd, Riverdene Business Park, Hersham, Surrey KT12 4RG.

Code: 9904/B

INTRODUCTION

One of the difficulties in getting older is that it becomes harder to place childhood events in their proper chronological order. That is why I'm not really certain as to which particular pier I saw first, Saltburn or Cleethorpes.

I definitely remember going to stay with my late maternal grandmother at Stockton-on-Tees, and travelling from there by train to Saltburn. We also had a week's holiday in the resort one year. What my memory recalls of the pier is its landward end café, and admission notices for the anglers who wished to fish further out into the sea. Not being fishermen, I don't think we ventured any further than the café.

As for Cleethorpes, it happened to be the adjacent seaside town to Grimsby, where our family moved when I wasn't yet seven. What struck me most about this part of the East Coast was just how far the tide went out, something especially noticeable when you've got a small pier that becomes somewhat overwhelmed by the sheer quantity of sand.

Naturally it hadn't always been like this. Before and immediately after the war, Cleethorpes pier had extended for a more than respectable 1,200ft. Yet after being breached for defence purposes in 1940, the isolated seaward section was damaged by storms, and deemed in peacetime not worthy of restoration. Thus local residents were faced from then on with a structure just 335ft long, while Leicester City Football Club made use of some of the salvaged material to help them build a new stand at their Filbert Street ground. When I eventually saw Norwich City play there in the early 1980s, I tried to imagine what might have been.

My recollections therefore do not go back to what one can describe as the 'Glory Days' for seaside piers. Indeed, the same can be said with regard to Saltburn. For the aforementioned holiday was in 1969, four years after the pier underwent its last major repair job. And 1971 saw a pile lost, showing the true condition of the Victorian structure.

The 1970s were to be a decade of frustration for the seaside pier. Saltburn and Cleethorpes were only two of those whose futures had been called into question – a similar story can be written about Clevedon, Brighton West and Bangor, and I could go on.

It was the events of that decade, and the concern shown by local inhabitants who feared the loss of their piers, that led to the formation of the National Piers Society in 1979, under the Honorary Presidency of the Poet Laureate, the late Sir John Betjeman. A launch in central London at the Connaught Rooms drew much publicity, getting the society off to a good start. Members weren't only preservationists, but also historians and engineers, along with those involved in running their own pier(s). Such people welcomed the formation of a powerful pressure group, which would serve as a clearing house for those with a common interest.

Twenty years later, the tide has undoubtedly turned. True, some piers still face a fight for their survival in an increasingly competitive leisure industry. And the older they get, the harder – and costlier – it will be to revive them. Yet today we can talk of piers that have been successfully restored (Clevedon, Penarth and Swanage were reopened in 1998 alone), rather than simply hope that there will be a white knight on the horizon.

Why has there been this shift towards recognising the value of piers? To be truthful, there are a thousand and one different reasons, including the creation of the Lottery and its provision of money for heritage projects. Yet were it not for the growing public interest in piers, I doubt whether Lottery applications would have stood a chance. People, thankfully, are looking back as well as forward, realising what might be lost to future generations if steps aren't taken now. This involves reminiscing about the Glory Days, when a pier was an essential facet of the British seaside.

Whether its walking to a summer show, eating candy floss in the breeze, or landing by paddle-steamer, piers bring the memories flooding back. This was brought home to me following a relevant article in the *Hull Daily Mail*, and I received many phone calls and letters from people who had a pier-related story to tell from their youth, which led them to want to know more.

Hopefully *Glory Days: Piers* will itself help stimulate a few recollections of what was, and what – if the society has its way – will be once again.

Tim Mickleburgh
Grimsby
January 1999

▲ SOUTHBOURNE – A pier that didn't last long: it opened in 1888, was wrecked by storms in 1900 and 1901, before being pulled down in 1909 on safety grounds. *Wayne Walters Collection*

◄ ROTTINGDEAN – One of the shortest-lasting piers, it opened in 1896 as a 'station' for the Brighton & Rottingdean Seashore Electric Tramroad. The railway lasted until 1901, the pier being pulled down in 1909. *Author's Collection*

SALTBURN – This fine pier is reached by a cliff railway. It was opened in 1869, but already reduced in length to 1,250ft by the time of World War 1, thanks to storm damage. *John Haddaway Collection* ▲

SALTBURN – After a public inquiry in 1976, the end trestles were removed leaving a 681ft pier. Reopening took place two years later. *Author's Collection* ▶

CLEETHORPES – A view inside the present (second) pavilion, dating from 1905. The picture was taken in the following decade. The pavilion was altered in 1968, then remained unchanged until transformed into a nightclub – Pier 39 (named after a modernised steamer pier in San Francisco) – in 1985. *Richard Riding Collection* ▶▶

Interior of Pier Pavilion, Cleethorpes.

RELIABLE SERIES 04.

BRIGHTON, WEST PIER –
The paddle-steamer
Brighton Queen is seen
landing at the newly-
extended west side landing
stage in the early 1900s.
Richard Riding Collection

BRIGHTON. — WEST PIER, WEST SIDE, SHOWING "BRIGHTON QUEEN" AT LANDING STAGE.

BRIGHTON, WEST PIER –
A traditional Edwardian
view of the pier, before the
bandstand was replaced by
a concert hall in 1916.
Richard Riding Collection

WEST PIER BRIGHTON.

D.45755. CLEVEDON: PIER ENTRANCE.

CLEVEDON – This was always one of the finest English piers, even though lacking much in the way of amusements. The ornate Toll House typifies both the resort and pier.
Richard Riding Collection

CLEVEDON – After two spans fell into the water during testing in 1970, the pier had a fight for its survival. It beat a demolition order thanks to a public inquiry and reopened in 1989, except for the ornate 1894 pavilion. This early 1998 view shows the pavilion being added once more to the head; not long after (May 1998) the official reopening took place.
Andrew Monro Collection

1. ORIGINS AND EARLY DEVELOPMENT

GREAT YARMOUTH, JETTY – How does one distinguish between a pier and a jetty? Usually the latter are smaller in scale, with a distinct lack of entertainments. But that at Great Yarmouth is of important historical significance – the first jetty arguably goes back to 1560, with that illustrated here dating from 1808, prior to the earliest seaside piers. Today's jetty was built by the Dutch in 1953.
Author's Collection

▲ It is appropriate that the National Piers Society has a close relationship with the Paddle Steamer Preservation Society, known throughout the boating world for its ownership of PS *Waverley*. For the origin of seaside piers is very much tied up with the history of boats and shipping, and the need for vessels to have somewhere to land.

At the very beginning, man sailed on lakes and rivers sheltered from the severest of storms. Consequently, boats simply went from the shore. Yet once people began to explore the high seas, harbours were required.

Initially these were natural, but this acted as a limit on the growth of shipping. For not everywhere on a busy trade route was a suitable site to receive boats. Thus harbours became increasingly man-made, built exactly where traders wanted them to be.

It is these artificial constructions that can be said to be the ancestors of piers as we know them. They date back a very long way: archaeologist Avner Raban claimed (in 1981) that the harbour at Caesarea was the first to have free-standing breakwaters, which it had in 13BC. It was thus 'the first modern harbour in history'.

Or was it? Evidence has it that the Egyptians, Romans, Greeks and Cretans were long skilled at harbour building. What have been called 'great harbours' were constructed at Alexandria, Carthage and Ostia.

The ancient harbour of Alexandria is particularly interesting. Not only did it contain the Pharos Lighthouse, one of the seven wonders of the world, but a sketch shows that it was divided in two by a great embankment. Boats sailed between, through gaps left at either end. Yet even this harbour wasn't the original on this site, replacing as it did a Cretan harbour that had breakwaters up to a length of 6,500ft.

The collapse of the great empires led to many of their engineering works falling into decay. But one shouldn't forget the importance of the early Mediterranean harbours in paving the way for what came very much later.

'Modern history' could be said to begin in the late 1700s. Sir John Betjeman is recorded as saying that the sea

Pavilion and Pier, Weymouth

◄ WEYMOUTH,
COMMERCIAL / PLEASURE
– Is this the oldest ever
pier? Whether the original
structure dates from 1812
or 1840, the pier is certainly
one of the earliest. The
picture shows the
passenger landing stage
built for the Great Western
Railway in 1888-9, and was
taken shortly after the
pavilion was built in 1908.
Author's Collection

◄ WEYMOUTH,
COMMERCIAL / PLEASURE
– A close-up view of the
Pavilion Theatre, again
shortly after construction.
Some have discounted this
structure as not deserving
to be called a seaside pier:
facilities such as this show
why it merits listing.
Richard Riding Collection

The Pavilion and entrance to Pier. Weymouth.

◄ YARMOUTH, ISLE OF
WIGHT – Opened 1876, the
pier is still built of wood,
unlike most that have been
developed over the years.
Repair work began in late
1993 to ensure its survival
for another 40-50 years.
Andrew Monro Collection

was considered to be 'a very ugly thing' in the 18th century. 'You were not supposed to look at it; and it was dangerous, and connected with trade.' Being 'in trade' was looked down upon by the aristocracy, especially in the early years of the Industrial Revolution that was to establish Great Britain as the 'Workshop of the World'.

For a nation with a maritime background and heroes like Drake, it isn't surprising that the 'fear' of the sea didn't last. In fact the success of spa towns like Bath helped to dispel this dread, and it wasn't long before the fashionable moved on to what have been called 'seaside watering places', Brighton and Scarborough being two early examples. Jetties were constructed for these early promenaders, who were happy to walk out to sea while keeping their feet firmly on terra firma (or should that read 'decking'?).

Such jetties often had a more functional purpose in mind, serving as they did as landing stages for boats. Inland transportation wasn't anything to write home about before the coming of the railways, with the best roads still

RYDE – Arguably the oldest pier of them all, dating from 1814, and still in being today. It actually consisted of three piers in one, with a tramway pier (1864) and railway pier (1880) added alongside. The tramway closed in 1969, leaving gaps between the railway and promenade piers. The picture was taken in the Edwardian era.
Wayne Walters Collection

Ryde from Ryde Pier

RYDE – Another historic view of particular interest, in that the Victoria Pier (pulled down 1924) can be seen on the left of the picture. Today one can still travel by train from the pier-head station, though the motive power is electric multiple-units rather than steam.
Wayne Walters Collection

arguably those that remained from Roman times. Until the likes of Turnpike Trusts and Telford and McAdam, there had been little attempt to build decent highways since then.

Canals of course helped to make matters better for industry. But with a low maximum speed, the comparatively few leisure travellers often chose the sea route as the best means of getting from coast to coast, even if the mileage involved in a journey was far greater. Hence the use of jetties.

According to Walvin's *Beside the Seaside*, piers (the word pier is really interchangeable with jetty in these historical times) were in being at Great Yarmouth and Margate as early as 1800. Indeed, Great Yarmouth Jetty arguably goes back much further, with a 1560 building date given by one authority. Lord Nelson reputedly landed here, and thus the structure became known locally as Nelson's Jetty. A new jetty was built here in 1808.

Five other piers of sorts have a history that dates before 1810: the first Ilfracombe pier (1678), Chatham Sun Pier

ARROCHAR – Situated at the end of Loch Long, the pier replaced an old jetty in 1850. It finally closed in 1977, though remains can still be seen, including the 'T'-shaped head.
Author's Collection

BRIGHTON, CHAIN – Not the first seaside pier as is sometimes erroneously claimed, but opening in 1823, it is certainly one of the oldest. It was destroyed by a storm in 1896.
Richard Riding Collection

on the Medway (1765), Hull on the River Humber (c1801-03), Westminster Pier on the Thames (pre-1806) and Troon in Ayrshire (c1808). Yet though of interest to researchers, such constructions certainly aren't anything like the piers we know today.

When, therefore, did the humble landing jetties/piers become fully-fledged seaside piers? The answer in fact is not that much later. The predecessor of the present Weymouth Commercial/Pleasure pier had a building date of 1812, according to a Betjeman article, though another source gives 1840 as the year of its construction. No uncertainty exists so far as Ryde Pier is concerned. A Parliamentary act was passed in 1812, and plans drawn up by John Kent of Southampton. Work began the following year, with the then 1,740ft pier officially opened on 26 July 1814.

More well known than either Weymouth or Ryde was Brighton Chain Pier, designed by Captain Samuel Brown RN. Proposals for a pier or jetty in this large Sussex resort had existed since 1806, but the Brighthelmston Suspension Pier Company wasn't formed until 1821. The Chain Pier officially opened two years later, having cost £30,000 to build.

It wasn't the first of its type: Leith Trinity Chain had opened on 14 August 1821, with the same designer. Smaller (640ft rather than 1,134ft) and cheaper (costing just £4,000), it is looked upon as being the template for its famous Southern counterpart.

Brighton Chain, a terminus for packet boats going to Dieppe, became a popular attraction. Facilities included a camera obscura, a regimental band, small kiosks, shops, shower baths and a weighing machine. It gained the patronage of William IV (reigned 1830-7), who subsequently was to knight Captain Brown, and inspired a song:

But of all the sweet pleasures that Brighton can boast,
A walk on the Chain Pier delighteth me most.
That elegant structure, light airy and free,
Like a work of enchantment hangs over the sea,
The hey derry-derry – be this the toast here,
George the 4th and Old England, the People and Pier!

It would be interesting to know its tune! Incidentally, with George IV dying in 1830, the words obviously date from not long after the pier opened.

I should, perhaps, point out that chain piers (there was later to be one at Seaview on the Isle of Wight, and also on the Thames at Chelsea, Cadogan) were so called because of their similarity to a suspension or chain bridge, early examples of which saw the light of day in the 1820s. That across the Menai Strait to Anglesey dates from this time. The main difference was that instead of taking you direct from A to B, a chain pier would convey you from A to sea!

The 'pier' craze began to gather momentum and the 1830s saw a number of structures erected. That at Southend saw its foundation stone laid in July 1829 by the Lord Mayor of London, after attention had been drawn to the fact that there was no proper site for boats to land between Harwich and Tilbury when the tide went out. In 1830 600ft of decking was opened to the public, with extensions taking its length to no less than $1\frac{1}{4}$ miles by 1846. No other town was to have a seaside pier that was so long, even overseas.

Also in 1830, another Essex pier opened, at Walton-on-the-Naze. Originally just 330ft long, it was later extended to 800ft. Herne Bay Pier followed in 1832, to the designs of Thomas Telford. It extended for 3,613ft, and a 'baggage line' that carried the luggage of travellers is credited with being the first ever pier railway.

Sadly, none of these post-Ryde constructions survive today. Brighton Chain was destroyed by a severe storm in 1896, with Leith Trinity Chain suffering a similar fate two years later. Southend got a replacement pier in 1890, while the present pier at Herne Bay is the third on that particular site. Walton still has a pier, and for nine years actually boasted two. The original structure was, however, washed away in 1880.

Southampton Royal, opened on 8 July 1833 by the Duchess of Kent and Princess (later Queen) Victoria, does survive, and this is now the second oldest pier in being. Alas, its condition today makes it hardly recognisable as a traditional pier. In its heyday the pier served as a ferry terminal, built for the Harbour Commissioners, as well as

WINTER GARDENS AND WELLINGTON PIER, GREAT YARMOUTH.

GREAT YARMOUTH, WELLINGTON – The older of the two Great Yarmouth piers, this was reconstructed in the early years of this century, opening in 1903 complete with wooden pavilion. The council also had the Winter Gardens transported from Torquay, and though land-based, these formed part of the pier complex. This pre-World War 1 view shows both pavilion and Winter Gardens.
Author's Collection

The Pavilion Wellington Pier.   Great Yarmouth.

GREAT YARMOUTH, WELLINGTON – A close-up view of the Pier pavilion, which survives today and is used for shows.
Richard Riding Collection

Beaumaris, General View

boasting a pavilion and other leisure attractions.

Deal was another early example, constructed in 1838 to the designs of J. Rennie. Yet it was never a success, with a mere 250ft of the planned 445ft ever seeing the light of day. Like Herne Bay, the present pier is the third the resort has known.

Into the 1840s, and Wales enters the pier age with a short structure at Beaumaris. This opened in 1846, the same year as Lowestoft South Pier. Remarkably, both piers can still be seen today, albeit in a highly modified form: Beaumaris was rebuilt in 1872 and extended before the end of the century, whilst Lowestoft South is currently part closed, with an area blocked off and marked by a 'dangerous structure' notice.

Beaumaris Pier has benefited from facing the Menai Strait, rather than the open sea. Consequently, it has not been so much at risk from storms. Lowestoft South actually forms part of the town's harbour, and therefore fills an essential role. Its future is thus more assured than the majority of piers, which merely serve a leisure market.

BEAUMARIS – The first Welsh pier, seen here at a distance in pre-World War 2 days with its pavilion. It had been extended in 1895, and consists of two parts – stone at the shoreward end and iron at the seaward end. *Author's Collection*

BEAUMARIS – A close-up view, showing the pavilion and landing stage, from which boats still travel. Snowdonia can sometimes be seen, though is often shrouded in mist as here. *Wayne Walters Collection*

After these two structures came the Wellington Pier at Great Yarmouth, a town already possessing an historic jetty. It opened in 1853. Great Yarmouth went on to become the first resort with two piers, following the opening of the Britannia Pier just five years later.

Yet in between these dates, a construction at Margate had marked an important development in pier building. For it was the first iron pier.

Early piers had been built either out of stone (Lowestoft South) or more commonly timber. Wood, however, though able to carry high loads for a time without failure, is a material which is vulnerable to decay. Thus to use cast iron was certainly a major step forward.

Margate Pier (known locally as the jetty to distinguish it from a harbour wall misleadingly called the pier) opened in 1855, being also the first pier designed by Eugenius Birch. He went on to design a further 13 structures, of which seven survive today, namely Blackpool North, Aberystwyth, Brighton West, Weston-super-Mare Birnbeck, Eastbourne, Hastings and Bournemouth. For the record, he

MARGATE JETTY – Into the 1920s, and structurally little has altered. Sadly, the pier was virtually wrecked by a storm in 1978, though remains of the pier-head could still be seen until 1998.
Richard Riding Collection

MARGATE JETTY – Confusingly called the jetty, to distinguish it from a nearby harbour wall, it was the first iron pier ever constructed, opening in 1855 as a replacement for a wooden structure known as the Jarvis Landing Stage. It was also the first pier designed by Eugenius Birch. This view dates from shortly before the outbreak of World War 1.
Richard Riding Collection

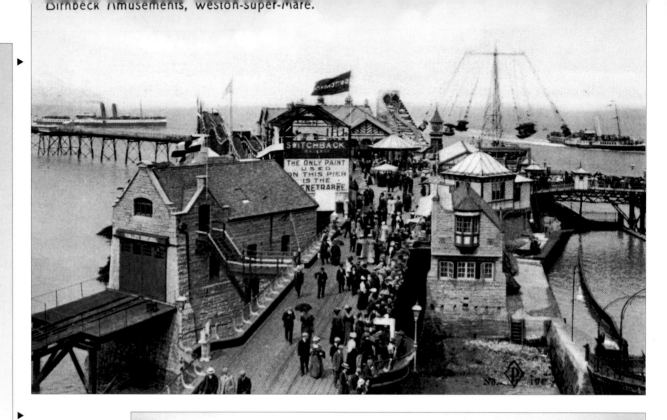

WESTON-SUPER-MARE, BIRNBECK – An unusual pier as it 'includes' Birnbeck Island, a small group of Bristol Channel rocks. The low-water jetty (seen here on the left) closed in 1910 and lasted just until 1923. The amusements largely ended in 1933 when the funfair opened on the Grand Pier.
John Haddaway Collection

WESTON-SUPER-MARE, BIRNBECK – Closed and derelict in the late 1990s, the pier is still used by anglers. New owners took over in 1998, and it is hoped that restoration can begin.
Andrew Monro Collection

The Pier, Southport

When the sea is not at Blackpool.

◄ SOUTHPORT – The second longest pier in the UK, this Edwardian view shows only that part of the neck which goes over the water. It is interesting to read the comment from the card's original sender in 1906.
Author's Collection

was additionally responsible for piers at Deal (the second pier), Lytham, New Brighton, Scarborough (North), Hornsea and Plymouth (Hoe). Sadly, Margate Pier isn't one of the lucky ones, being virtually destroyed by a storm in 1978 – part of the wrecked pier-head can still be seen, however, and there are occasional calls for something to be done about it.

The oldest iron pier remaining today, and the fifth oldest of all, is Southport. Opening in 1860, a year after Swanage's wooden pier, it overtook Herne Bay to become the second longest in the UK at 4,380ft. Though now reduced in length (to 3,633ft), the pier still claims this honour.

By the time Southport was doing business, piers were on the verge of being a national phenomenon. Its construction really does mark the end of the 'early days'. The idea that resorts would benefit from one of these man-made 'spindly creatures' on legs had taken hold, except perhaps in Scotland.

◄ SOUTHPORT – The pier has changed little over the years, though it is now threatened. A stroll along its 3,633ft length will help convey what a traditional pier is like. Not surprisingly, there has been a pier railway since the early days, 1863 in fact. This is the oldest surviving iron pier.
Author's Collection

24 BOURNEMOUTH. — On the Pier. — LL.

True, north of the border there was one pier at Leith, putting paid to the myth that piers aren't something one should associate with this part of the UK. And the 1820s saw piers built at Inverary, Banavie, Inverfarigaig, Kilmun and Invermoriston; the 1830s brought piers at Largs and Dunoon; and the 1840s structures at Balloch, Bowling, Fairlie, Garelochhead, Inversnaid, Kirn, Luss, Rosneath, Stornoway, Strone, Tarbet and Wemyss Bay. Overall, I have record of approximately 200 Scottish piers. But they were (and are) really landing jetties, similar to the constructions which preceded Ryde. Only the later Portobello (1871-1917) is listed alongside its English and Welsh equivalents, though it must be said that others – chiefly Dunoon, of the piers that still exist – almost make it, and shouldn't be ignored by researchers.

For one thing, Scottish piers can show us something of what a pier once was, before the pleasure lovers got their way in the great pier building age.

BOURNEMOUTH – A pre-World War 1 view, showing a traditional steamer calling. The pier had recently (1905) been extended to 1,000ft.
Richard Riding Collection

BOURNEMOUTH – A view soon after World War 2, again with paddle-steamers alongside. A new pavilion (1960) was itself replaced in 1979-81.
Richard Riding Collection

A rough Sea at Deal.

DUNOON – With the disappearance of genuine seaside piers at Leith (washed away in 1898) and Portobello (demolished 1917), this is probably the finest Scottish pier still remaining. The first pier on the site was built in 1835, whilst the present 1898 structure incorporates an earlier 1867 design.
Author's Collection

DUNOON – A view from 1989, showing the car ferry leaving for Gourock. £175,000 was spent in 1980/81 on rehabilitating the central mock-Tudor buildings. *W. S. Foster*

◀ DUMBARTON CASTLE –
Opened in 1875 amidst
great ceremony, a gale in
1900 severely damaged the
structure, which was
abandoned eight years later.
Author's Collection

◀ SANDBANK OLD – Named
to distinguish it from the
'New' Military Pier, this
private structure on Holy
Loch, off the Firth of Clyde,
is used by Robertson's
Yacht Yard. It is seen in
1990. Scotland has many
piers like this. *W. S. Foster*

FOLKESTONE, VICTORIA – Though popular, this was never the most profitable of piers. Its most noteworthy feature was the 700-seater pavilion. Note the harbour wall immediately behind – this dates from 1807.
Author's Collection

The Pier from Leas, Folkestone.

FOLKESTONE, VICTORIA – Though just 683ft long, the impression here is of a longer pier. Perhaps if it had been so, success would have come more easily. Alas, the final remains were pulled down in 1954.
Richard Riding Collection

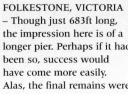

Egremont Pier and River.

Kyles of Bute, East from Tigh-na-Bruaich Pier

EGREMONT – The functional basis of piers as mere landing stages survived in the structures we describe today as 'river piers'. Those on the Mersey were the most impressive, even apart from the traditional seaside pier at New Brighton. Though Birkenhead (Woodside) and Seacombe (Wallasey) survive, along with Liverpool's famous Pier-head, sadly Egremont was not so lucky. Dating originally from 1835, though reconstructed out of iron in 1876, it was pulled down in 1946 after being badly damaged by a ship collision five years before. *Author's Collection*

TIGHNABRUAICH – This pier was built in the 1850s, though widely rebuilt before opening again in 1885. This turn-of-the-century view shows how close the resort, popular with yachtsmen, is to the Isle of Bute. The pier is still in being, and is used by PS *Waverley* amongst others. *Author's Collection*

2. THE PIER BUILDING AGE

The Glory Days for pier building were to last for over 50 years, from 1860 to virtually the outbreak of World War 1 (1914). Including replacement structures, 85 genuine seaside piers were constructed around the British coastline. The 1860s was the peak decade, with no less than 22 piers opening. The 1870s saw 19 such celebrations, the 1880s and 1890s saw 15 each, and the 1900s saw 12. Fleetwood (opened on Whit Monday 1910) and Burnham (1911) were the last piers of an historic era.

What, however, were the reasons for the popularity of seaside piers? The answers lie in social and economic history. We have already noted just how poor inland transport was in the early years of the 19th century. Matters were, however, to change dramatically with the coming of the railways.

There had been coal-carrying lines as early as 1550 abroad, and 1604 in this country. Horses formed the motive

SKEGNESS – The pier is seen immediately before World War 2, with the entrance having been modified to incorporate a café and shops. Note that much of the pier is over land, a fact that is more noticeable today since storm damage in 1978. *Author's Collection*

THE PIER, SKEGNESS.

FLEETWOOD – After a disastrous fire of 1952, rebuilding was necessary, and the 'New Super Pier' opened the following year. A further facelift took place in 1972; today the pier is chiefly noted for its vast Bingo Hall. *Author's Collection*

FLEETWOOD – The last of the 'golden age' of pier building, this pier has always been somehow overshadowed by its neighbours at Blackpool, a mere tram ride away. But this view of the entrance, dating from not long after the pier opened (1910), shows it had merit of its own. *John Haddaway Collection*

Victoria Pier, Fleetwood

power, if not humans themselves. Not until 1804 did
Richard Trevithick succeed in building a steam locomotive
that was capable of haulage, with the initial regular steam
passenger service being a one-mile section of the
Canterbury & Whitstable Railway which was inaugurated
on 3 May 1830. By the middle of the following decade,
speeds of 70mph had been reached.

Thus the framework for a communications system
capable of transporting millions of people at a decent speed
existed. And thanks to the efforts of engineers,
entrepreneurs and 'navvies', Britain acquired a rail
network which left few places of any size more than a
handful of miles from a railway station. Track mileage in
fact rose from less than 2,000 in 1840, to over 15,500 in
1870.

If railway companies weren't responsible for actually
building the piers (as they had been at Cleethorpes thanks
to the Manchester, Sheffield & Lincolnshire Railway), they
were more than happy to carry the multitudes who were
wanting to go to the seaside, and hence on a pier. Private
individuals organised their own trips, as did societies. The
ordinary traveller also benefited from an act of 1844, which
compelled railway companies to run at least one train a
day in each direction that stopped at all stations and gave
passengers travelling third class a seated and covered ride
at no more than a penny a mile. These were known as
'Parliamentary trains'.

To travel anywhere, though, costs money and requires
time. This was no problem for the aristocratic seaside
goers, nor for the increasingly affluent middle classes who

started to patronise many resorts. But the ordinary worker had little in the way of surplus income or leisure time to spend on going to the sea. Until, therefore, something was done about this, there would be a limit as to how much the advancing number of new resorts could grow and how far the working classes themselves could benefit from an improvement in the standard of living.

Factory Acts were passed from 1833 onwards, serving to reduce the length of the working week for different groups of people, particularly women and children to begin with. Annual summer breaks came into force, with the famous 'Wakes Weeks' being a feature of Northern life. Built-up areas would become like ghost towns, as many would decamp *en masse* to the seaside at the same time.

The introduction of Bank Holidays helped to formalise the amount of leisure time available: four such days came into being following a Parliamentary act of 1871. It is significant that Hastings Pier was opened on the first August Bank Holiday in 1872, with Cleethorpes Pier following suit a year later.

Different towns, however, had different reasons as to why they expanded, or in some cases, failed to match the expectations of promoters who wanted to see them become a Mecca for visitors. It is worth while to look at a few examples, and see why some piers became more popular, and hence more financially successful, than others.

Weston-super-Mare Birnbeck had opened in 1867, and incorporated the small island of Birnbeck (little more than a collection of rocks in reality). Originally the pier consisted of a long iron section, together with a short westward jetty from the island. Because of a wide tidal range, the main pier was the highest in the country.

Paddle-steamers called right from the early days, and a wooden north jetty was added in 1872. A tramway was constructed to carry the luggage of passengers; by the 1890s it was estimated that the steamers were conveying up to 15,000 people a day. Many were day-trippers who toiled in the mines and steel plants of South Wales for a living. They made use of the facilities provided on the island, which included a switchback railway and pavilion.

Clevedon, however, was not so well placed. Though it became popular with merchants from Bath, the town

BRIGHTON, WEST PIER – A general view of the pier in its interwar heyday, showing both the concert hall and southern end pavilion. *Author's Collection*

NORTH PIER, BLACKPOOL

BLACKPOOL NORTH – The oldest, and finest, of Blackpool's three piers. A typical 1920s view, showing that orchestras remained a popular attraction.
Richard Riding Collection

BLACKPOOL NORTH – The bandstand, clearly seen here, was built in the 1870s as part of the pier-head alterations. It became the sun lounge before the onset of World War 2.
Richard Riding Collection

▲ didn't grow as much as had been expected. Engineer J. W. Grover had claimed that a look at Bradshaw (the railway timetable) would enable one to discover that Clevedon was on the route from London to South Wales. That just wasn't true. For the railway, built in 1847, was merely a branch line run by the Bristol & Exeter Company. Most express trains bypassed the town, whilst paddle-steamers were engaged mainly in taking passengers on excursion trips to places like Minehead, Chepstow and Ilfracombe. Their services did not form part of a main route between London and South Wales.

The town remained largely sedate, and the pier (erected 1869) did not become full of the popular attractions that were a feature of structures elsewhere. It was, in fact, too slender to house anything substantial. A pavilion, none the less, was added in 1894, when the original pier-head was replaced.

Yet with its elegant legs, built from discarded wrought-iron railway lines, Clevedon was, and is, one of the most attractive piers ever built. Not for nothing was it ultimately to gain Grade II* listing, and be described by the Environment Secretary as 'an exceptionally important building warranting every effort to preserve it'.

Skegness might be considered as somewhat isolated from large areas of population, being situated in a less densely inhabited part of Lincolnshire, a county that cannot boast a city/town with over 100,000 people. Yet once again thanks to the railway, it became very popular with those escaping from the larger East Midlands towns of Derby and Nottingham. Indeed, the Skegness Pier Company had been set up by the Earl of Scarborough in 1877, who five years before had been instrumental in bringing the railway to Skegness.

As the pier building age developed, the structures themselves gradually became more elaborate. Arguably the greatest pier ever had been constructed at the start of this period, the Birch-designed Brighton West. Work commenced in 1863 and by the time it officially opened (6 October 1866), the pier extended for 1,115ft. There were two square kiosks at the entrance, two octagonal kiosks

BLACKPOOL CENTRAL – Though the Central Pier is most prominent in this view, the North Pier and the 'pier in the air' (Blackpool Tower!) can also be seen. Blackpool is one of the few resorts to have weathered the 1960s/70s storm, and remains a Mecca for millions of entertainment lovers. *Author's Collection*

CENTRAL PIER, BLACKPOOL

BLACKPOOL CENTRAL – The shore end 'White Pavilion' dated from 1903, but was demolished in 1966 to make way for the Dixieland Palace/Golden Goose entertainment complex. Nothing, it seems, stands still in Blackpool! *Richard Riding Collection*

with minarets at its centre, and four octagonal kiosks at the corners of the pier-head platform. Also here were windshields and a rotunda screen. Gas-lit lamp columns around the perimeter were decorated with entwined serpents, supposedly a motif taken from the music room of Brighton's Royal Pavilion. Widening of the pier took place in 1893, when the southern end pavilion was constructed.

By then Birch (1818-84) had sadly passed on – the pier remains his masterpiece, a monument to the glory days of pier building, and even 'Britain's finest structure' according to Napoleon III.

The West Pier had originally cost £27,000, but there were two piers whose costs were to run into six figures, namely Weston-super-Mare Grand and Brighton Palace.

Just as Brighton West was to be the resort's second pier, Weston-super-Mare Grand was also not the first such structure in its particular locality. Birnbeck Pier had been successful, as we have already seen. Yet it was felt by some to be a long way from the town centre, and, most importantly, the railway station. By simply making their progress to the nearest beach, trippers would miss the joys of pier life completely.

Plans for what eventually materialised as the Grand Pier were announced in 1880, but schemes fell through. Building eventually commenced on 7 November 1903, and the 1,080ft-long pier, together with pavilion, opened on 11 June 1904. The pavilion measured 150ft by 90ft, with a 62ft by 23ft stage. It was capable of drawing crowds of 2,000, who were able to enjoy everything from opera, ballet and Shakespeare to boxing and music hall.

A further 1,500ft-long low-water extension with timber landing stage was completed by 1906; at one time there had been talk of a one-and-a-half-mile pier, longer than Southend. However, the problems caused by tides and strong currents put paid to plans to run a regular passenger service to Cardiff, and records note that only three boats ever tied up there. The extension was demolished between 1916 and 1918, apart from 120ft beyond the pavilion.

£200,000 had apparently been originally subscribed, and the final cost reportedly came out as £120,000. But even this didn't match the £137,000 expended on Brighton's Palace Pier, the town's third. Sadly, all three were not open concurrently.

For the Marine Palace & Pier Company, established 1889, had only been given permission to erect a new pier on condition that the Old Chain Pier was removed. Thus the fledgling company purchased Brown's historic structure, chiefly so that they could pull it down. Yet as we've seen, it was storms which finally put paid to the Chain Pier. This helped the company to save money, despite the claims for compensation for damage caused by the wreckage.

From the day work began to the opening of the seaward end pavilion, 10 years elapsed – the longest time spent on constructing any individual pier. 1,760ft long, it didn't fully open until 3 April 1901, though it should be noted that apart from the pavilion, the pier had been doing business two years previously.

Oriental in design, there were onion domes and horseshoe arches, hung with coloured lights. The pavilion contained a 1,500-seater theatre, with other facilities including dining and grill rooms, along with smoking and reading rooms. Smoking rooms might seem strange today, yet it wasn't that long ago when tobacco use was something to be encouraged. In any case, piers have never been the home of the politically correct!

As if the pier wasn't grand enough, a further pavilion was added in 1910 at its centre. Brighton Palace therefore became one of the most architecturally significant piers: it is only the brilliance of the West Pier which has stopped many from singing its praises.

None of Blackpool's three piers matches either of Brighton's newest constructions so far as grandeur is concerned, though I would argue that Blackpool North does come reasonably close, at least in comparison with Brighton Palace. Blackpool, however, reigned supreme from the 1890s onwards in being the only British resort that had three genuine seaside piers. I add the word 'genuine', as both Morecambe and Great Yarmouth had seaside jetties in addition to two piers.

Blackpool North was and is the oldest of the three,

◀ WESTON-SUPER-MARE, GRAND – The pier's opening. The pavilion seated 2,000 people, and it was intended that the pier's full length would eventually be 6,600ft, second only to Southend.
Wayne Walters Collection

BLACKPOOL SOUTH – Turn-of-the-century view of what was then known as the Victoria Pier (renamed 'South Pier' in 1930). The pier had opened only in 1893, including a Grand Pavilion at the seaward end. *Author's Collection*

VICTORIA PIER, BLACKPOOL Copyright

BLACKPOOL SOUTH – Later, interwar shot of a pier that changed very little until an entrance pavilion was added, by the 1930s. *Author's Collection*

New South Promenade and Victoria Pier, Blackpool

WALTON-ON-NAZE FROM PIER PAVILION.

ELECTRIC TRAM CARS.

◄ WALTON – The present (second) pier was extended in 1898 to a length of 2,600ft – today only Southport and Southend are longer. This pre-World War 1 view shows the original electric tramway which lasted until 1935, when it was replaced by an unusual battery-operated car. *John Haddaway Collection*

◄ WALTON – A modern view, showing to the full the large undercover amusement arcade at the shoreward end. Sadly, though the railway was reopened with a diesel engine in 1948, the service ceased some time in the 1970s. Today a rail-less 'train' takes passengers to the head, where sometimes PS *Waverley* calls.
Richard Riding Collection

BOSCOMBE – Traditional view of a pier that was to change much in the late 1950s, when the neck was reconstructed in concrete. One of the earliest structures to be municipally controlled, with the council taking over its ownership in 1904.
Richard Riding Collection

BOSCOMBE – This view prior to World War 2 gives a good indication of the pier's iron work. *Author's Collection*

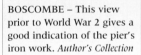

Boscombe from the Pier Looking West.

dating from 1863. Blackpool Central (confusingly to later historians, it was called the South Pier to begin with) opened in 1868, whilst Blackpool South (the shortest and least attractive of the three, though not completely without merit) didn't make an appearance until 1893.

Residents of Bournemouth might wish to claim parity with Blackpool, as there have been three piers within the area of the old Corporation. Yet one goes by the name Boscombe, and the other Southbourne. This latter construction has long since disappeared, having been pulled down in 1909 on safety grounds after a mere 21 years.

Ironically, some of the later piers were built for similar reasons to the oldest structures, as they served as landing stages for a steamer service. The Coast Development Company Ltd had been formed in 1898 by a merger of Belle Steamers Ltd and other local concerns: they were succeeded in 1905 by the Coast Development Corporation

Ltd. Whatever the name, this body was responsible for three East Anglian piers: Southwold (1900), Lowestoft Claremont (1903) and Felixstowe (1909). Of these, Felixstowe was the longest, extending for about half a mile, and including an electric tramway along its north side from the shore to the pier-head.

Mention here must additionally be made of Walton-on-the-Naze Pier, substantially rebuilt in the 1890s thanks to the efforts of the Walton-on-the-Naze Pier & Hotel Co Ltd. For this became one of the constituent companies of the Coast Development Company while construction work was going on.

Meanwhile, it is important to realise that seaside piers weren't being built just in the UK. They were starting to appear in many foreign countries, particularly the United States. Indeed, more piers were ultimately constructed there than in any other nation, including our own. This

The Steel Pier, Atlantic City, N. J.

▲ isn't surprising, when one considers the greater amount of coastline involved. Some of the piers 'across the pond' lacked the grace of their English counterparts admittedly. Nevertheless, one shouldn't get jingoistic. For in Atlantic City, New Jersey, no less than eight piers have existed over the years, a world record for any town or city.

The first, Georgia Avenue, was built in 1881 by the West Jersey & Atlantic Railroad Company, showing that the
▶ influence of railways in pier development wasn't solely a British thing. Alas, the wooden structure lasted for only two months before being destroyed by storms. Howard's Pier (named after a Colonel of that name), opened 1882, fared little better, with a replacement structure necessary by the following year. In 1889 this was sold to the city council, who demolished it in order to extend the famous boardwalk.

Later pier buildings were to be more fortunate, with three piers open today. These are Central Pier (formerly Applegate or Young's Pier), Ocean One (successor to the famous Million Dollar Pier) and Garden Pier. Remains of Steeplechase Pier and Steel Pier can also still be seen. No trace, however, exists of the renowned Heinz Ocean Pier, constructed in 1886 on iron pilings sunk by hydraulic method. This made it the first non-wooden pier of the resort. It got its name in 1898, when taken over by H. J. Heinz, the pickle (or beans!) millionaire. The pier was

TOTLAND BAY – Built in 1880, the facilities included a small shore end amusement pavilion, and steamers used to call. The pier is overlooked by the splendid Totland Bay Hotel, seen here in the Edwardian era. *John Haddaway Collection*

TOTLAND BAY – The Isle of Wight pier has changed owners several times since the mid-1970s, the amusement arcade being damaged by fire. The current owner purchased the pier for just £19,500 at auction in 1998 – its main facility is a shore end café. *Andrew Monro Collection*

open all the year round, with free admission. Estimates give a lifelong total of 50 million visitors during the Heinz years, which sadly came to an end following a wartime hurricane. Too badly wrecked to restore, demolition took place in January 1945.

Another US town with more seaside piers than Blackpool was Santa Monica. In all, five were built, including the Long Wharf, which was originally constructed in 1891 by the Southern Pacific Railroad for commercial purposes. Yet tourists used to fish and eat at its restaurant, with the 4,700ft-long structure being the longest in America. Sadly, its seaward end was pulled down in 1916, followed by complete removal in 1921. By then four other piers had been constructed: Municipal, Ocean Park, Venice and Looff. The latter is today considered to be part of the Municipal Pier (it was erected immediately adjacent to it), the only survivor as the century nears its close.

Continental European piers 'began' not long after those in the USA. Trouville in France, built of wood in 1889, is the oldest I've come across. It was, alas, destroyed during World War 2, as was Nice. Not long after Trouville came Blankenberge in Belgium, which gained a pier in 1895, to be followed by Scheveningen in Holland. Other European piers can be found in Italy, Germany, Poland, Bulgaria, Switzerland, Denmark, Norway and Austria. And further afield, I have record of structures in Malaysia, South Africa, Argentina, Singapore, the Falkland Islands, New Zealand, Australia, Canada, the Maldives, Russia, Peru and even Uruguay.

Nevertheless, it is probably right to portray piers as being somehow British in character. After all, they were conceived here, and were more popular in countries that either spoke English or had a British connection than elsewhere.

The pier building age came to a sudden halt, and the reasons for this require examination. One possible reason can be safely ignored – the outbreak of World War 1. There were no pier openings after Burnham, meaning that the three years (1912 to 1914) directly before the conflict were pier-less.

NICE – Appropriately built off 'La Promenade des Anglais', the short, elaborate pier was a victim of World War 2.
Author's Collection

Arguably the most straightforward explanation is that all places wanting piers already had them. This viewpoint certainly has a lot going for it. For bearing in mind the structures that had been pulled down or washed away, in 1914 no less than 82 fully-fledged seaside piers graced the British coastline. Some places did remain immune to their charms, with Mablethorpe (Lincolnshire) and Whitley Bay (Northumberland) being two notable examples. Yet elsewhere, such had been the enthusiasm for pier building that a town the size of Hornsea with a population then of just 1,500 was once going to have two piers! Even though one scheme did fall through, a pier was constructed at nearby Withernsea.

Towns without piers tended in general to fall in areas where few people lived, and where transport access was relatively poor. Cornwall on the other hand did have its decent-sized towns and railways, and thus one might have expected it to boast more than Falmouth Pier (Prince of Wales), a structure not even regarded as worth listing by some. Yet Cornwall was and is remote from much of Britain, with harbours helping to fulfil a similar function to piers in other parts of the country. The 'Banjo Pier' at East Looe, in reality a stone cob, is proof that the essential functions of more traditional piers weren't being ignored.

I've referred in the previous chapter to the structures in Scotland. They weren't seaside piers, but given a greater number of visitors, might well have been. As for the East Coast of this part of Britain, the paucity of even landing jetties can be explained by the existence of harbours which carried out a similar role.

Another reason cited for the end to pier building has been their increasing cost. We've already seen than it was costing upwards of £100,000 to build a structure on the grandest scale. No doubt this would have deterred many investors, along with the reality that their new structure would be facing competition from the piers that had long been there. It was much harder to build a market to the same extent as before, what with the prime sites taken by earlier builders. That's probably why some of the later constructions weren't the financial successes that their predecessors had been. To give an example, Folkestone

Victoria had opened in 1888, with £44,000 spent to build its 683ft length. A 700-seater pavilion proved to be popular, as was the pier itself. Yet no profits were recorded until 1898, and the founding company eventually leased the pavilion to Keith Prowse & Company Ltd. They brought variety artistes like Lillie Langtry (associated with King Edward VII) and Dan Leno to the pier – seat prices increased to as much as five shillings (25p) for one of the latter's performances. However, the pier still didn't pay, and the lease for the whole structure was transferred to two local businessmen in 1907.

The trouble was that running costs hadn't been properly accounted for. When one is dealing with a structure as vulnerable as a pier, ever at risk from the sea, maintenance is higher than for an equivalent structure inland. Sufficient sums must be put to one side on an annual basis, otherwise difficulties mount up, and owners can be faced with a large-scale restoration programme that they can't afford from a year's budget. Economising on repairs is certainly a short-sighted approach to pier management.

Of course, there was nothing to prevent speculators from erecting more basic piers, as the Coast Development Company had done in East Anglia. The public, however, appeared to be wanting more entertainment facilities, with the novelty of walking out over the sea less important than it had been. They were not so prepared to stay on the beach all day, what with charabanc trips making it easier for the holidaymaker to visit different resorts on the same day. If your holiday time was limited, then you certainly wanted to make the most of the leisure you were lucky enough to have. Thus, unless you really needed a pier/jetty to land boats on, there wasn't much point in erecting such a simple design – you wouldn't make money from it!

So as the Edwardian era passed away and the storm clouds of war approached, piers had become part of the traditional seaside. New constructions might have ceased, but in terms of development, piers still had a long way to go!

FALMOUTH, PRINCE OF WALES – The only seaside pier in Cornwall, and even then it is not counted as such by some authorities. Named after the future King George V, who laid the foundation stone two years before the structure opened in 1905. *Author's Collection*

PRINCE OF WALES PIER, FALMOUTH

FALMOUTH, PRINCE OF WALES – This pier is similar to Beaumaris in that the pier is partly piled and partly made of stone. At 510ft long, it remained largely unaltered until reconstruction in 1951. Today there are shops across its entrance. *Richard Riding Collection*

Prince of Wales Pier, Falmouth. 6135

3. FROM WAR TO THE PLEASURE DAYS

World War 1 was the bloodiest conflict that man had yet seen. Few families escaped unscathed, such was the casualty total, with thousands dying on a single day of battles like the Somme which claimed over a million victims.

At home, however, how did the war affect leisure time, and piers in particular? Obviously the sheer number of young men overseas would have an impact; similarly the entry of many females into new areas of (better paid) employment, including munitions factories.

Southampton Royal Pier had acquired a railway, with its own station erected next to the pontoon. By 1913, repairs were deemed necessary by the Harbour Board's engineer because of decay. Yet trains ceased to operate for the duration of the 1914-18 conflict, and the service wasn't resumed in peacetime.

The cessation of transport services seems to have been part of a common pattern. Herne Bay's steamers stopped running, with cars from its tramway being first used as a temporary shelter and then sold for scrap. After a period of closure, the pier didn't reopen until hostilities had ended. As for Morecambe Central, it is recorded that here too pleasure steamers stopped in 1914. Meanwhile over at Ramsey Queen's Pier on the Isle of Man, a place further away from any fighting, the same year has gone down as being the last great season of passenger steamer traffic.

The only surviving chain pier, Seaview on the Isle of Wight, was another that closed for much of World War 1. And when it did at last reopen, in 1919, the regular steamer services that had formed part of the pier's operations were not revived. Skegness did remain open throughout the war, but to reduced business.

A couple of piers were badly damaged. Ramsgate Marina, a short (550ft) structure constructed by the famous pier-building firm of Head Wrightson from Stockton-on-Tees, had already started to decay by 1914, and was duly closed. Hopes of a postwar renaissance were severely hit when the pier was affected by both fire and a ship collision in 1917. The final blow occurred the following year, when a drifting mine exploded underneath the piling. This left the pier beyond repair: it was finally pulled down in 1930 by the Ministry of Transport. Lowestoft South, a concrete structure, was the other wartime victim, damaged by bombardment. Thankfully, however, it did survive.

Lee-on-Solent Pier was used on at least one occasion during this time, when HM King Albert of the Belgians landed here. The king walked along Esplanade Road, and the Marine Parade. Meanwhile, the local borough council took over the pier in Aberystwyth on a lease in 1915.

Considering the size and importance of the town, it is more surprising to note what happened at Brighton West. For, in 1914-16, right in the middle of the war, much building work was carried out. The pier was further widened at its centre, with a new concert hall replacing an earlier bandstand. At Colwyn Bay too there seem to have been positive developments, with the building of the Bijou Theatre apparently taking place the same year as Brighton West acquired its new concert hall. The new theatre seated 600 people, and was thus a major attraction in a resort of this size.

At Eastbourne there were no construction works. However, the Knuts Kamp Komedy Kompany (the misspellings are correct!) from the Summerdown convalescent camp performed on the bandstand. And gossip said that if you were sufficiently talented to get into the Blue Boys Concert Party, you had a much longer spell of recuperation than you really needed.

Therefore the war's impact varied from town to town, and it is pointless to make sweeping generalisations so far as piers are concerned.

The same is true with regard to the interwar years. Those well-versed in social history are only too aware that, for many people, this era is categorised by severe economic

RAMSGATE – Though the Kentish pier was completely demolished in 1930, the reverse of this card is dated 1946. The practice of resorts selling 'out of date' cards is thus not new! The pier actually closed as early as 1914.
John Haddaway Collection

THE PIER, RAMSGATE.

RAMSGATE – Seen in better days: the 250-seater pavilion can clearly be seen, though the switchback railway had already been removed (1897). Other facilities included a camera obscura, of the type still in operation in Edinburgh.
National Piers Society

downturns. Three are particularly significant: the post-World War 1 slump, caused by having to readjust a market to non-militaristic ends, whilst finding work for millions of returning soldiers; the mid-1920s period associated with the General Strike and the lock-out of many miners; and the Great Depression of the early 1930s, symbolically triggered by the Wall Street Crash in America.

For the ordinary man and woman, slumps were signified by job losses, and at their peak, over three million jobless were recorded. This excluded many who were not officially registered, and amounted to more than 20% of the recorded workforce. With benefit cuts a factor, it is easy to imagine Britain as a country where leisure activities would struggle for survival.

Yet as if to prove the economists wrong, many piers thrived; so much so that it is probably true to say that the 1920s and 1930s were their real 'glory days' for entertainment.

This might sound somewhat illogical. However, the economic misfortune, though undoubtedly dreadful, didn't

BEACH AND PAVILION, COLWYN BAY.

Sea Front and Pier, Colwyn Bay.

COLWYN BAY – Two views showing the pavilion of 1934 shortly after it had been built to replace an earlier fire-damaged structure. Since the Paxmans bought the pier in 1994, they have done sterling work to try and convert it to its former glory. Visitors were admitted from the summer of 1995, and the pier is open all year round. Sadly, however, renovation of the pavilion remains a long-term target. The owners had applications for Lottery funding turned down on the ground that they are private individuals. *Author's Collection*

hit everyone evenly and didn't hit everywhere. There was a sharp contrast between the regions reliant on traditional 'heavy' industries like coal, and those areas which were growing as a result of new and expanding industries based on technological innovations, cars and chemicals being two of the most prominent. What is more, in between times of recessions there were booms: that was one reason why the stock market collapse was so dramatic, because there was further for it to fall than ever before. And once recovery had set in, unemployment steadily declined to a third of its highest level. There was thus plenty of scope for piers to expand and become the people's palaces we think of.

One new pier was built, namely Weymouth Bandstand. It had been the subject of an open architectural competition held under the supervision of the Royal Institute of British Architects. Twenty-six designs were duly submitted, and the winner was a Mr V. J. Wenning from London. Opened in 1939, the pier was very short – less than 200ft in length. Yet as befitted a prize-winning design, it was certainly very modern.

The seating capacity of its bandstand enclosure was put at 2,400, with a third of this number under shelter. The lack of cover caused problems when it rained, and the shelters became somewhat overcrowded! In all, 3,000 tons of concrete and 180 tons of steel were used in the pier's construction, along with five and a half miles of steel conduits, 2,500ft of two-colour neon tubing and 1,200 electric lamps. Ten large illuminated glass panels were grouped either side of the 'entrance loggia', and depicted well-known local beauty spots.

Weymouth's Commercial/Pleasure Pier was also developed in the 1930s. A new reinforced concrete pier some 1,320ft long and varying between 40ft and 100ft wide was officially opened by the Prince of Wales (later King Edward VIII) on 13 July 1933. This replaced an earlier wooden structure, and its north side was constructed to provide a promenade complete with shelters, dressing rooms for bathers and an elaborate diving stage. The latter facility was simply for ordinary members of the public to use – the distinction is made

The Pier, Clacton-on-Sea.

because of the popularity of exhibition divers in certain resorts. They gave themselves grand titles, often pretending to be professors, and caused much delight amongst their seaside audiences.

Worthing Pier saw many changes from after it had been purchased by the local authority in 1920 for £18,978. This municipalisation of ownership happened to several piers, and is a trend worth mentioning. At Worthing extensive repairs were carried out in 1925, and a new shoreward end pavilion opened the year after, seating 1,063 people. Costing £40,000 to build, it became the home of the only full-time all-year-round municipal orchestra. The pavilion was followed by a Southern Pavilion in 1935 (this replaced a Victorian building that had been destroyed by fire), built at a cost of £18,000, and a central amusement pavilion which opened two years after that. A windshield was also constructed down the length of the pier.

Weston-super-Mare saw what was arguably the most magnificent interwar pavilion built on any pier. Again, it resulted from an earlier structure being destroyed by fire.

CLACTON – A long-time Mecca for entertainment, as can be seen in this prewar view, showing concerts, dancing, bathing and something called Skeeball available. The more traditional pier walker is served by the 'Belle' steamers that call – one is visible on camera.
Wayne Walters Collection

THE PIER, CLACTON-ON-SEA, FROM THE AIR.   138

CLACTON – Postwar developments maintain Clacton's position in the entertainment league. But the emphasis has changed on Britain's second widest pier to fair rides, including a roundabout and a big dipper.
Wayne Walters Collection

MORECAMBE, WEST END – The interesting thing about this view of Morecambe's second pier (after the Central) is that it shows how similar land-based shelters/bandstands etc were to those incorporated into traditional pier design. Piers thus were very much buildings of their time. *Author's Collection*

West End Pier, Morecambe.

MORECAMBE, WEST END – A postcard actually sent during 1916, when World War 1 was at its height. So far as the West End Pier was concerned, 1917 was the year of disaster as its impressive pavilion, seen here, was wrecked by fire. Alas, storms put paid to the pier for good in 1977, and despite award-winning plans for a new construction, 1978's demolition of its remains was the last anyone saw of the West End Pier. *Richard Riding Collection*

CLACTON – Pre-World War 1 view. Apart from the pavilion and new landing stage (1890s), there is little in the way of large-scale facilities. *Author's Collection*

The Pier, Clacton on Sea.

CLACTON – Into the 1920s, and the pier is on the verge of its great entertainment breakthrough. Here fishing and promenading appear to be the most popular activities.
Wayne Walters Collection

The Pier, Clacton on Sea.

PENARTH – Early view of the 1895 pier, showing the seaward end wooden pavilion that was destroyed by fire in 1931 and never replaced.
John Haddaway Collection

PENARTH – The fine shore end pavilion was added in 1927/28, and is thankfully still in being today. A restoration programme of the entire pier began in 1994, with the formal reopening taking place in May 1998.
Andrew Monro Collection

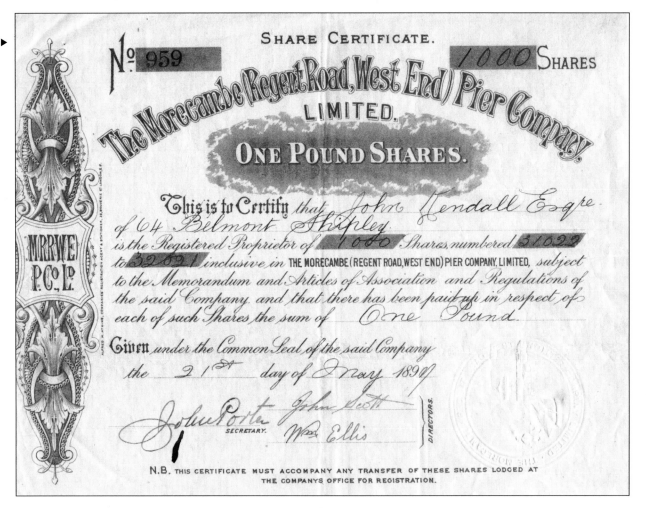

The new pavilion, opened in 1933, claimed to be the largest of its kind. Compared to what had gone before, it housed a giant funfair instead of the more traditional theatre.

The alterations at Clacton may not have given it a single building to match that at Weston Grand, but were certainly significant in that they helped create a pier that catered for the mass leisure market. These developments included the building of the Blue Lagoon Dance Hall (1922), a lifeboat house, the Crystal Casino, a children's theatre (entertainments were provided by Clown Bertram), a swimming pool and a new berthing arm. The pier was widened – only Southsea Clarence is wider.

Clacton Pier became synonymous with entertainment,

NEW BRIGHTON PIER.

one of the artists performing there being the future Lord Delfont, then a dancer. It marked the début of his theatrical career; he went on to become Chief Executive of First Leisure PLC, which owned a number of piers (including the three at Blackpool) in the 1980s and 1990s.

Work at piers elsewhere was not quite so spectacular. Southport got a new pavilion (1934), housing an amusement arcade, café and bar. At Penarth, a large impressive shoreward end pavilion was added, along with a concrete landing stage (1927-8). This was fortunate, as an older wooden pavilion, dating from 1907, was destroyed by fire on August Bank Holiday Monday in 1931. New pavilions appeared also on the piers at Sandown (1934), Morecambe Central (1935-6), and Colwyn Bay (1923 and 1934). Sandown's pavilion was in addition to the older pier-head pavilion, whilst that at Morecambe Central replaced an older fire-hit structure. Colwyn Bay's 1923 pavilion replaced one burnt down, and was itself replaced in 1934 after suffering the same fate.

A similar tale can be told at Blackpool North, again showing how vulnerable piers were to fires. The old Indian Pavilion was destroyed in 1921, replaced, badly damaged in 1938 (costs estimated at £30,000) and finally rebuilt by the following year. Eastbourne was luckier, with its shoreward end pavilion of 1925 a completely new building. It was used as a ballroom for many years, before becoming an amusement arcade.

Boscombe pre-dated the renovations of Weymouth Commercial/Pleasure Pier with renewal of its head in high alumina concrete in 1924-5 and 1927. It was one of the earliest marine structures to make use of this material, which was noted for its strength and early setting properties. The neck of the pier remained steel-framed until 1958-60, when that too was reconstructed using concrete.

Meanwhile at Southend, the Southend Pier Order was obtained in 1927, enabling the railway to be converted to double track: work was carried out from 1929 onwards.

MORECAMBE, CENTRAL –
The older of the two piers
in this northwest resort,
this sadly suffered a similar
fate to the West End Pier
when it too was demolished
in 1992. The pavilion seen
here was constructed in
1897/98, but destroyed by
fire in July 1933.
Author's Collection

MORECAMBE

MORECAMBE, CENTRAL –
Storms are an ever-present
threat to piers, as this pre-
World War 1 view shows.
Author's Collection

8427   *Rough Sea.*   *Morecambe.*

SOUTHEND – The longest pier in the world, that is of the seaside variety. The present structure opened in 1890; this picture shows it before the Prince George Extension was added in 1929. *Author's Collection*

SOUTHEND – Unlike Southport and Herne Bay (the second and third longest for much of the time), Southend has maintained its length. Yet it has been a victim of fires, the most recent being that which destroyed the shoreward end Bowling Alley in 1995, prior to this photo. *Author's Collection*

The reason for this expansion was the large increase in the number of those using the trains, up from 844,360 in 1913 to a figure approaching two million in 1925. Also under the order, a steamer extension was erected, named after Prince George who opened it in 1929.

Many of a certain age can still recall the old paddle-boats that landed at most piers, not just Southend. Take May Giles, now of Grimsby:

'As a child living 18 miles from Liverpool, the highlight of our day was to be taken on the workman's train to the city. It was cheaper – you had to be up early to catch it.

'Shopping in Liverpool was followed by the great excitement of going down to the Pier Head to catch either the *Royal Iris* or the *Royal Daffodil* to New Brighton Pier.

'Sailing on these ferry boats was to us as big a thrill as it would be to some people sailing on the *Queen Mary*. It was great – we never went under cover, but always watched the waves, and waited to alight at New

Brighton Pier. On then to the wooden floorboards, and down to the sands for our picnic amongst pools and rocks. If you were lucky you saw a crab.

'Our concerts took place on the pier. On one occasion, the comedian borrowed my new beret and twirled it round on a stick like some people do with plates.'

Skegness pier perhaps isn't one that you associate with shipping – the tide goes out a long way there! Nevertheless, in the late 1920s a triangular Skegness-King's Lynn-Hunstanton service was operated by the North Sea Steamship Company, with pleasure boats landing 7,000 people at the pier in a single year (1929). Sadly, as time went on, the water became insufficiently deep for the pier-head to be used by steamers.

Of the paddlers at Herne Bay, that most closely associated with the pier from the late 1920s to 1963 was the famous *Medway Queen*. Based at Strood on the River Medway, it frequently landed here, calling at Southend on the way. The *Medway Queen* was later to play a role in the evacuation of Dunkirk, being one of the 'little ships' that

NEW BRIGHTON – This view dates from the time the pier was taken over by Wallasey Corporation (1928), whose developments included a new pavilion. Sadly, the pier was pulled down in 1977, after permission was granted by the Environment Secretary. *Author's Collection*

Boating Pool, New Brighton.

Marine Palace Pier.   Brighton.

helped save so many lives. Today a society exists to fight for her restoration, and it is to be hoped that when she is seaworthy again, pier visits will form part of her operational schedule.

The short structure at Beaumaris found itself served by steamers belonging to the Liverpool & North Wales Steamship Company, *Snowdon*, *St Elvies* and *La Marguerite* being the names of three famous paddlers in the pre-World War 2 era. In the 1920s, the PS *Snowdon* was chartered by a local Sunday school for its annual outing to Llandudno.

Afternoon cruises regularly went in the other direction: from Llandudno Pier there were also day trips to the Isle of Man, and a timetabled service to Liverpool. These were run by the same company mentioned above, whose steamers continued to operate until the 2,326-ton *St Tudno* made her final sailing in 1962.

Yet like other piers, Llandudno's entertainments were just as much a part of the 'glory days' as these steamer services. In the 1920s the pier had what was arguably the best seaside orchestra in the country. Noted conductors appearing at the pavilion included Sir Malcolm Sargent, Sir Edward German, Sir Adrian Boult, Sir Henry Wood (of promenade concert fame) and Sir Thomas Beecham.

A policy change in the 1930s saw classical concerts switched to the pier-head pavilion, whilst the main pavilion became the venue for a series of summer shows. Jimmy Jewel appeared in the first such show, staged by impresario Hugh Stanhope, and entitled 'Joymill'. Others to appear on the pier over the years were Ted Ray, Cyril Fletcher, Vera Lynn, David Nixon, Jimmy Edwards, Hughie Green and Jimmy Young.

St Annes too had its orchestra, which had originally begun as a ladies' orchestra: Mr William Reed was the first male conductor, in 1930. Leading entertainers used to appear, including Gracie Fields and George Formby; later stars were pianist Russ Conway and comedian Bob Monkhouse. George Formby, incidentally, will always be associated with piers, thanks to his song *The Wigan Boat*

HERNE BAY – There have been three piers at this resort, the present one dating from 1899 and incorporating much of the short second structure. The electric tramway, whose rails are seen here, lasted until the onset of World War 2. Once the third longest pier in the country (at 3,387ft), storms destroyed the main neck in 1978. The remains today stand isolated as a reminder of what the pier used to be. The modern 'sports' pavilion, opened 1976, remains widely popular.
John Haddaway Collection

Express about the mythical structure at Wigan. Yet though the subject of jokes, as piers are not supposed to be found inland, there was actually a pier (in reality a coal tippler) on the site next to the Leeds-Liverpool canal. With today's Wigan Pier tourist centre, there's nothing to laugh about now!

Piers in the 1920s and 1930s adapted to the trends and fashions of the day. Brighton Palace hosted Charleston teas and charabanc parties, some held in the Marine Palace Tea Garden on the pier's roof. It was estimated that 45,000 passed through the pier's turnstiles on a single 1939 Bank Holiday.

Hastings Pier can be added to the list of those with an orchestra. What is more, it often broadcast on the radio, giving pier music a much wider audience than would otherwise have been the case. No doubt the listeners sat back and recalled past seaside holidays as the melodies filled the airwaves. A local repertory company, Harry Hanson's Court Players, also performed here from 1930 onwards. One of the two pavilions that Hastings then

LLANDUDNO – This is only a partial view, as the promenade end of the pier is not visible here. A fine structure, it is seen at the start of the 20th century before further pier-head building in 1905.
Author's Collection

LLANDUDNO – A view dating from the same period, showing the promenade entrance. The tall building is the Grand Hotel.
Wayne Walters Collection

boasted (an additional one had been constructed in 1926) became an intimate theatre, another was adapted to take an Art Deco frontage. This was in keeping with the spirit of the age.

Meanwhile, at Colwyn Bay, those enjoying the musical concerts were not only served refreshments, but also given free use of newspapers and periodicals. It is not known, however, what the musicians on stage thought of this practice! Bingo and opera remained popular, along with wrestling, old-time dancing and tea dances.

Sadly, there were some losses to balance the overall impression of growth. We have already considered the fate of Ramsgate Marina; Dover Promenade was another casualty to record.

It had opened back in 1893, after the Dover Promenade Pier Company had been formed five years earlier. After being bought by the Admiralty in 1913 for use as an additional landing stage, it was leased again as a pleasure pier in the postwar era. But though steamer trips to Hastings brought in visitors and helped the pier to become a popular attraction in the early 1920s, extensive repair work was deemed to be necessary if the structure was to survive. As this was not thought justified on economic grounds, the pier closed and was demolished in 1927. No remains exist to show us where it was.

Ryde Victoria was also demolished in the 1920s, though its days had clearly been numbered for some time. A replacement pier constructed in 1864, it remained in the shadow of its longer, and older, neighbour. The local borough council had acquired the pier for a mere £1,000 in 1914, in order to obtain a right of way. An Act of Parliament allowed for its demolition, the final traces being washed away in 1924.

Yet there are always exceptions to every rule. Thus it can be said that in general, the interwar period formed part of the 'glory days' for the seaside pier. Whether through dancing, watching shows or travelling by paddle-steamer, their position as an integral part of the coastal holiday was crystal clear. Indeed, why else had there been so much in the way of development if not to cater for more and more visitors? So as the summer of 1939 drew to a close, what could happen to take away the trippers' dream?

The Pier, Felixstowe.

TRAMS
TO THE END OF PIER EVERY FEW MINUTES
FARE 2D CHILDREN 1D.

DOVER, PROMENADE –
The pier, opened in 1893,
was named to distinguish it
from the Admiralty and
Prince of Wales piers, which
are categorised as being
structures of the
railway/steamer variety
only. This Edwardian view
clearly shows how the
entrance was overshadowed
by the Burlington Hotel.
Author's Collection

DOVER, PROMENADE –
An overall view from the
same period. The seaward
end pavilion was designed
by J. W. Adcock, and added
(in 1899) after the pier had
been open for several years.
Richard Riding Collection

THE PROMENADE PIER, DOVER

ST ANNES – The splendid Moorish pavilion, seen shortly after it opened in 1904, was sadly destroyed by fire in 1974, causing the pier company to go into liquidation.
Author's Collection

ST ANNES – Refurbished in the early 1990s, the pier was repainted in green and white, giving a neat and tidy appearance. The seaward end was removed after a fire in 1982 that also destroyed the Floral Hall.
Author's Collection

4. WORLD WAR 2

World War 2 certainly had a major effect on Britain's seaside piers. Just as with the 1914-18 conflict, that which was to last from 1939 to 1945 left its scars on the traditional way of life. And this time, piers were deemed, literally, to be in the firing line.

It was widely expected that the German troops would try and invade these shores. Considering that this country had previously been protected by the Channel for many years, this was a threat to be taken seriously. However, the approach to trying to defend Britain against onslaught left something to be desired. Where would the invaders land at least some of their forces when they had managed to cross the sea? Why, on the end of a pier of course! Today, this sounds a ridiculous notion. Piers are such an obvious landmark of any resort, being near to built-up areas in order to attract the crowds. Consequently, those looking out for the enemy would immediately see them were they to arrive there. No, a sophisticated naval force would find themselves a secluded bay somewhere, miles away from a crowded town like Brighton, Blackpool, Great Yarmouth or Bournemouth. It was said that piers would have been only a secondary source of landing, but the whole notion is worthy of deep scepticism.

Sadly, it seems that those responsible appear to have underestimated the resourcefulness of the German forces. And so the order went out for piers to be 'sectioned'; that is, have part of their decking forcibly removed. Thus if there were to be an invasion, troops would find themselves on a man-made island, isolated from the shore.

Most piers on the east and southeast coasts were therefore breached. These were the structures in towns felt to be most at risk, due to their proximity to the Continent. Remember that France had fallen, increasing the potential danger. Some piers elsewhere were to suffer the same fate. Indeed, a report by Admiral Sir Frederick C. Dreyer recommended that most West Coast piers should be breached just in case.

At Eastbourne, in May 1940, the Army arrived shortly after 10pm during the middle of a show (Clarkson Rose in 'Twinkle') with orders to blow up a specific section. They were persuaded to wait until the entertainment was over, though explosive charges were placed by sappers while the audience left the pier. The staff were given three days to remove what they felt was necessary, items that could be damaged in any blast. However, it was eventually decided simply to remove a large piece of decking by means other than explosion.

The whole of Lee-on-Solent was warned to keep all windows wide open when the pier was being dynamited, to save the resultant blast from wrecking them. People were supposed to keep away from the vicinity of the Lee Tower and Pier Street, on safety grounds. Yet not everyone did so. An eyewitness report spoke of a mother pushing a baby in a pram, who was lucky to escape unharmed. She had to run away speedily in order to escape the flying debris. The pier wasn't so fortunate, of course, with the head separated from the rest of the structure. This was redecked, using planks that had been blown overboard.

Things were different in Blackpool. Apparently, it was suggested that the three piers needed to be breached for the reasons already outlined. This was met with the answer that they wouldn't mind the Germans landing at any one of the pier-heads. Puzzled as to this lack of concern, the official enquired further, to be told that if guns were placed strategically at the entrances facing down the piers, they'd have the invading forces immediately in their sights! Apocryphal or not (for wouldn't pier buildings get in the way?) the piers in this famous northwest resort escaped sectioning and the problems this could later cause.

The war seems to have put paid to the steamer services described in the last chapter. Boats would be a prime target for attack, while fleets were sometimes needed for military services: we have already noted the role played by PS

Sandown Bay.

Medway Queen in the famous evacuation at Dunkirk. Pier railways suffered too. At Herne Bay, traffic had grown to such an extent that a 15min service during peak hours (9.30am to 6pm) was considered to be necessary. But on 3 November 1939, the railway ran for the very last time. Unlike after World War 1, there was no subsequent reopening, with the cars ending up sold for scrap. At Felixstowe, a similar thing happened. Services were suspended following the outbreak of war, and this suspension eventually became permanent, making Felixstowe another trainless pier.

The railway at Southend Pier didn't close, but was used by the Navy to carry wounded and able-bodied men from ships, in addition to stores and equipment loaded at the pier-head. The pier as a whole was under Naval control, being known as HMS *Leigh* – Leigh is a suburb of Southend. It was fortified with pill-boxes and anti-aircraft guns, actually beating off an attack from the Luftwaffe (the German air force) during the period of the so-called phoney war.

Southend wasn't the only pier to be commandeered.

Lowestoft Claremont had its isolated section linked by a Bailey bridge once the invasion threat had lessened, becoming an Army Training Centre. Cowes Victoria on the Isle of Wight was also taken over by the Navy, along with the rest of the parade. This was despite the pier being just 170ft in length, and thus of limited use for landing purposes.

The Navy took over Bognor Regis pier too, which like that at Southend acquired a special name, HMS *Patricia*. It became an observation station. Yet the naval involvement didn't prevent it from being sectioned. Similarly, Hastings Pier was used by the armed forces for training. And as for Worthing, it was the shore end pavilion which assumed a military position, being converted into a recreation centre for troops.

Shanklin Pier on the Isle of Wight became uniquely important, because of the oil conveyed by PLUTO (Pipe Line Under The Ocean) for the Normandy landings. The pipeline actually ran along the pier, and was divided into two sections so as to cross the gap left by the pier's earlier breaching.

The Pier, Eastbourne.

EASTBOURNE – Traditional pre-World War 1 view, showing the seaward-end theatre complex which had been added in 1899-1901. This replaced an older construction (1888). The pier was taken over by Leisure Parcs PLC of Blackpool in 1998, after being under the ownership of First Leisure PLC. *John Haddaway Collection*

CLAREMONT PIER, LOWESTOFT.

Claremont Pier, Lowestoft.

◄ LOWESTOFT, CLAREMONT – By the 1930s, a pavilion had been added, along with buildings on the 'T'-shaped pier-head: these were part of immediate pre-World War 1 development. Alas, though a new pavilion (built 1950) still caters for visitors, the decking beyond remains closed today on safety grounds. *Author's Collection*

SANDOWN – Into the 1920s, the pier had altered surprisingly little: the pier-head pavilion (built 1895) was not joined by the centre pavilion until the mid-1930s. Today only the latter construction survives, with the pavilion seen here replaced from 1971 onwards; it was by then fire damaged.
Richard Riding Collection

However, it should be said that the section to France wasn't laid until after the invasion scare, and that only a very little of the small amount of oil pumped across the Channel came from the Isle of Wight. Indeed, that which did started from Sandown, because the Shanklin line failed.

Yet unlike the 'sectioning' concept, it would be wrong to decry the working of what was a hugely complex scheme, and which might have brought great benefit to many people. Incidentally, relics from the PLUTO days can be seen in a Shanklin exhibition.

The two piers that fared worst because of the war were those at Minehead and Deal.

Minehead had always been a popular place for shipping, ever since it opened in 1901. It had four landing stages, with steamers calling on a regular basis. Alas, the War Office decreed it to be in the line of fire of a nearby gun battery. Thus, in 1940, it was pulled down so that the guns could have a clear line of sight. Campbell's, the owners, were given £90,000 in compensation, but this was used to improve their steamer fleet, rather than being spent on a replacement structure once the conflict was over.

In the mid-1990s, Minehead Pier 2000 Association was formed. It was hoped that a new £5 million pier could be built, using money from the National Lottery millennium fund. Sadly, the association's application for finance was rejected.

The second pier at Deal was equally badly affected. The Dutch ship *Nora*, anchored a mile off-shore, was hit by a drifting mine which blew a hole in its stern. The *Nora* was taken onto land, but a rising tide lifted the vessel from the beach and caused it to crash continually against the pier. Finally the *Nora* was driven right through the pier, destroying 200ft of ironwork. Left a wreck, the pier structure was subsequently demolished by the army, as with Minehead, to give coastal guns a clear line of fire. Only the entrance toll-booths remained.

Overseas, we've already mentioned that Nice and Trouville in France were victims of World War 2. The jury is out as to whether Scheveningen in the Netherlands fits into the same category. For on 26 March 1943, the iron and wood structure, opened in 1901 by Prince Hendrik,

Minehead Pier.

45803. MINEHEAD: THE PIER & STEAMER.

SHANKLIN – Pre-World War 1 view, taken before the first pavilion was built (1909), and prior to the removal of the landing stage (1915).
Author's Collection

HASTINGS – Always popular at Christmas time, the pantomime in the early years of the century could be seen for as little as 4d (approximately 1.5p) or as much as 2s 6d (12.5p).
Author's Collection

Pier Extension and Bandstand, Hastings.

HASTINGS – A fine Birch-designed pier, its shore end pavilion was built in 1926, with an Art Deco façade added the following decade, when this image was produced.
Wayne Walters Collection

◄ HASTINGS – Piers were popular by night, with illuminations often used to good effect, as this enhanced view of the entrance shows. *Author's Collection*

SCHEVENINGEN – Opened in 1902, this view of the pier was produced less than a decade later. The pier was wrecked by fire in 1943 under mysterious circumstances, but a replacement was opened in 1961 by Prince Bernhard. *Author's Collection*

TROUVILLE – Dating from 1889, this is the oldest European structure I have a record of. It was destroyed in World War 2. *Author's Collection*

20 TROUVILLE - REINE DES PLAGES - Départ du bateau au Hâvre

Promenade Pier, Plymouth. 650.

PLYMOUTH, HOE – This was Birch's final pier, just 480ft long. A 2,000-seater pavilion added in 1891 was its main attraction, used for anything from dancing to wrestling. *Author's Collection*

Pier and Staddon Heights, Plymouth

14443

PLYMOUTH, HOE – This card is postmarked 1922, the year when steamers stopped calling at the pier. The pier was never a great success, probably because the city is not noted as a seaside resort, and was finally pulled down in 1953. *Author's Collection*

SCARBOROUGH, NORTH – With the card date-stamped 1904, this view cannot have been taken that long before the storm of 6 January 1905 which destroyed all except the entrance pavilion. It was never a great success, probably because it was in the 'wrong' bay of this two-bayed resort. *Richard Riding Collection*

CLARENCE GARDENS & PIER, SCARBOROUGH.

SCARBOROUGH, NORTH – Postcards such as this appeared soon after the fatal storm, and it was claimed by wags that their sale caused more money to be made out of the pier than ever before! The entrance building survived until 1914. *Author's Collection*

Scarborough. — The Wreck of the Promenade Pier.

mysteriously burnt down. It is still not known whether this was a genuine accident or whether the Germans can be blamed. Whatever, the superstructure was removed the following January, and the leftover piles were taken away in 1945.

Aside from these extreme cases, other piers suffered in a war that had a long-lasting impact. The bombardment of Southampton Royal was just part of the city's overall suffering. A parachute mine in fact exploded, tearing up a large area of the decking. The pier's buildings also housed French refugees, and it played a significant role leading up to D-Day.

Southsea Clarence was another bomb casualty, being badly damaged on the night of 10 January 1941. Southsea by itself might seem a strange target for the enemy, but the seaside resort is of course adjacent to Portsmouth, where there had long been a naval base. It and Southampton, a major shipping port, were prime targets for enemy forces.

Thankfully, at least both Southsea Clarence and Southampton Royal were to see a new life after the war, especially the former which was to be extensively rebuilt. However, the bombing of Plymouth, another city known for its naval history, was to seal the fate of the Hoe Pier.

It had opened in May 1884, four months after the death

of its famous designer, Eugenius Birch; Plymouth Hoe was the last pier of the 14 he designed. A mere 480ft long, a large pier-head pavilion was added in 1890/91, capable of accommodating up to 2,000 people. The pier became reasonably successful, though truth be told, its location worked to its disadvantage. For though Plymouth was a reasonably-sized city by the coast, it was more noted for having a naval dockyard than for being a seaside resort. And by the 1930s, the pier was losing money, with receivers appointed in 1938.

During World War 2, Plymouth became an obvious target for the German bombers. After a particularly heavy raid in March 1941, the pier was left a twisted wreck. Payments were made by the War Damage Commission, but these went to buy out the debenture holders and to pay the £4,754 cost of demolition, a task carried out in 1953. Plymouth had a development plan, but alas, a new pier was not part of the postwar proposals.

Thankfully Redcar on the East Coast did outlive the mine that exploded nearby. Yet this helped to weaken the decaying neck, which proved even more vulnerable to storms. Thus by the time the war was over, just the pavilion and 45ft of decking beyond were left.

Mine damage also hit the pier at Southwold, though the structure was thankfully rebuilt, opening in 1948 after £30,000 worth of rebuilding work – a not inconsiderable sum for postwar Britain, especially as the structure was never particularly elaborate.

Elsewhere in East Anglia, Lowestoft South joined the list of bombarded piers. The main pavilion/reading room was badly wrecked, and the bandstand also hit. Meanwhile the famous West Pier at Brighton which had been developed during World War 1 wasn't so lucky in World War 2. As well as being sectioned, mines and sandbags were placed at strategic intervals along the decking. The octagonal kiosk to the west of an amusement arcade was in fact very badly impaired as a result of what was considered to be excessive loading, and had to be pulled down. Indeed, though the pier opened for business in 1948, many say it never really recovered from its wartime days.

That in fact was a typical story for many piers. They may have survived whatever the enemy or the weather threw at them, but found themselves very much weakened thanks to this 'double whammy'. For like other parts of the nation's infrastructure, including the rail network which had played such a role in their original growth, running repairs were not exactly a priority while there were opposition forces to defeat. Even when the guns stopped there was not going to be an immediate transformation of fortunes, especially in a country financially hard-pressed and still enduring much in the way of rationing and shortages. Come 1945, it sadly seemed that the 'glory days' were long behind us.

Let's not, however, conclude this wartime analysis on a gloomy note. Away from the more threatened eastern/southeastern quarter of Britain, the possibility of invasion wasn't so great. Which explains the situation at Fleetwood. Not the grandest of structures, improvements had been made to the pier in both 1930 and 1938. Then in 1942, a projection room was added, showing the popularity of cinema in the pre-television age, and that piers kept abreast of leisure advancements.

Southport too was partially open, at least so far as dancing was concerned. Mrs Alice Calvert of Hebden Bridge is one who remembers these times:

'I recall way back to the war days, and a lovely holiday at Southport with my family. I was 24 and my niece was 14. A part of every day was spent at the tea dance. My niece couldn't dance, and was too shy to get up, in case she couldn't do it. Anyway I assured her I felt sure I could teach her the waltz, then the foxtrot. By the end of the week she was quite competent and thrilled to bits. It was so precious, the memory has stayed with me loud and clear.'

An oasis of sanity you might say, and an indication of what piers had been, and, optimistically, could be once again. But for the moment, there was the small matter of an enemy requiring defeat.

SOUTHWOLD – This is one of the later 'plain' piers built primarily for steamer landings. These, however, ended in the 1930s, though a landward end pavilion, built in 1936, remained popular. The picture shows the pier at its original 810ft length; storms have reduced it since 1979 to just 150ft. *Author's Collection*

SOUTHWOLD – The 1936 pavilion has become much altered over the years. Since this photo was taken, part was altered to become a public house (1960), with the first floor reopening (1988) as a function room. Today this includes a ballroom, stage, bar and raised seating area. *Richard Riding Collection*

HYTHE – At 2,100ft, this is the seventh longest pier in the country today and is famed for its railway, opened to passengers in 1922. It was never an amusement pier, though the Hythe Sailing Club used to have a clubhouse on the pier-head.
Richard Riding Collection

THE HARD, HYTHE. MJ549.

HYTHE – The railway is still the main feature of the pier, from which ferries make the 12min journey to Southampton Town Quay every half hour throughout the day.
Andrew Monro Collection

Harbour and Beach, Lowestoft

◀ LOWESTOFT, SOUTH – A stone pier built as part of the harbour in 1846, this is a fully-fledged seaside construction nevertheless. The impressive pavilion/reading room dated from 1891 and lasted until the late 1940s. It is seen here in the pre-World War 1 period. *Author's Collection*

◀ LOWESTOFT, SOUTH – Dating from the same era as the previous picture, this view is taken looking back to shore from the wider section which carried the pavilion. Though there were two later shoreward end developments (1956 and 1975), today only single-storey amusement buildings have much to offer.
Richard Riding Collection

5. THE LAST HURRAH?

With the continued effect of wartime decay, it is not surprising that the 1950s was to prove the most disastrous decade for seaside piers. Alum Bay, Rhos-on-Sea, Lee-on-Solent, St Leonards, Seaview and Tenby Royal Victoria were fated to join Plymouth Hoe in oblivion before the 10 years were out. And not far behind were the structures at Lytham and Cowes Victoria, which went in the early years of the 1960s.

Dealing with the casualties alphabetically, we start with Alum Bay, a short (370ft) landing pier used at one stage by steamers, and housing a café. But the last boat called in 1920, and the structure closed on safety grounds five years after that. Yet even though a span collapsed as early as 1927, the shore side remained in operation until just before World War 2, with the whole village used for military practice during the conflict. Remains of the pier lasted until the late 1950s, and a warning sign cautioned people of the dangers of intruding on the few girders that were left. Today, however, there is no trace of the iron pier, though a small floating landing stage caters for launches taking trippers to the Needles headland.

Cowes Victoria had ceased to be used by the Navy and needed much in the way of structural repair, the making good of fire damage. Yet no such funding was available. Consequently the pavilion was demolished in 1951. An attempt by a private purchaser to restore what was left proved to be unsuccessful, and sadly the wholesale demolition took place in 1961, with a limited section of substructure surviving for a further four years.

After the war, a Captain Cutler made valiant attempts to revive the ferry which went from Lee-on-Solent to Cowes, using a powerful ex-RAF launch with two engines each of 200hp. Yet when Cutler left the area, the service closed down.

Ownership of the pier had passed to Gosport Council, who declined to use the compensation money they had received on rebuilding the structure. Sadly, it was spent elsewhere, and the pier was demolished on the council's orders in 1958. Even a smaller landing jetty was dismantled.

Lytham Pier became another postwar victim. It had closed in 1938, except to anglers. Repairs were made to the entrance building, but these proved to be insufficient to stop the rest of the pier's condition from deteriorating. Despite a petition signed by 2,500 residents, the council chose to demolish what was becoming a public eyesore. Owner Harry Kaniya was given £4,000 in compensation, a sum exceeding the cost of demolition (£3,320), which was carried out in spring 1960. The fourth oldest ever Birch-designed pier was thus no more.

Rhos-on-Sea was a genuine curiosity, having originally been constructed in 1869 at Douglas on the Isle of Man! A group of North Wales businessmen purchased the pier in 1895/96, and it was re-erected at its new site not far from Colwyn Bay, which wasn't to gain a pier until 1900. Rhos Pier, as it then was, became damaged by fire and was pulled down in 1954. As a footnote, it perhaps should be added that there were plans in the 1870s to relocate Teignmouth Pier to Paignton. Structural difficulties however put paid to this, leaving Douglas/Rhos as a unique example in the world of British seaside piers.

St Leonards Palace had gone before Rhos. It had been hit by both bombs and fire in the early 1940s, and after hostilities ceased, never reopened. Severe gale damage in March 1951 seems to have put paid to any lingering hopes that rebuilding might take place, and Hastings Corporation duly demolished the remains later that year.

The greatest tragedy of this postwar period was the pier at Seaview (one word instead of two since mid-Edwardian times). Navy-controlled in wartime, it was unfortunately in very bad condition when sold for a mere £775 in November 1947 as 'the only remaining suspension pier in England'. New owner Mr Figgins applied to the government for permission to restore the structure, but was apparently put

◄ ALUM BAY – An undated view showing this Isle of Wight pier which closed in 1925 on safety grounds, though the shore end survived longer. Steamer traffic had been infrequent since after World War 1 – before this, boats frequently ran to Southampton, Bournemouth and Portsmouth, and other Isle of Wight resorts.
Richard Riding Collection

◄ ALUM BAY – A bare pier, in a view showing the proximity of the famous Needles, the reason the first landing stage was erected here back in 1862. This iron structure dated from 1887 and replaced an older wooden one.
Author's Collection

HUNSTANTON – A traditional pre-World War 1 view, showing the 1890s pavilion destroyed by fire in June 1939. This pier, alas, was a victim of the 1978 storms, though a shore end amusement café still survives (in 1964 it replaced the entrance buildings shown here).
Author's Collection

HUNSTANTON – Another picture from the same era as the previous view, but showing the handsome pavilion in close up. There is no sign, however, of the later miniature steam railway, powered by a Bassett-Lowke engine and dismantled in the 1950s.
John Haddaway Collection

COWES, VICTORIA – One of the shortest piers ever built, it was just 170ft long when it opened in 1902. This view apparently shows the famous yachting week, shortly after two long shelters (1903) and a pavilion (1904) were added to the pier. *Author's Collection*

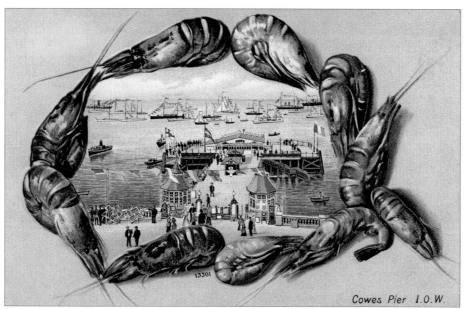

Cowes Pier I.O.W.

COWES, VICTORIA – This artist's impression is apparently based on the same photograph in the previous view. Sadly, the pier is no more, being largely dismantled in 1961. A slightly longer (250ft) Cowes Royal Pier lasted from just 1867 to 1882, but no images of it have been traced.
John Haddaway Collection

LYTHAM – One of the seven Birch-designed piers, this pier sadly is no longer in existence. It was built in 1865, with the pavilion added in 1892. This early 1900s view shows the pier probably at the height of its success. The pavilion had been converted to a cinema when it was destroyed by fire in 1927, and it was not replaced.
National Piers Society

LYTHAM – By 1938 the pier had closed except to anglers, though some repairs were made to the entrance buildings, seen here. Demolition was inevitable and, despite a petition, took place in 1960. Residents fortunately had the neighbouring pier at St Annes (the twin resort is often referred to as Lytham St Annes). *Author's Collection*

off by the form-filling and red tape involved. Residents, however, accepted that instead of spending the £6,000 needed on rebuilding, it would be better to construct a completely new pier. Eventually, though, the pier was sold again, to the owners of the nearby Pier Hotel. This time the sum involved had risen to £1,000.

Yet despite becoming (in 1950) the first pier to gain listed status under the Town & Country Planning Act, its future was imperilled by a series of storms. By the end of 1951, only the pier-head and around 100ft of decking were left. These were pulled down the following year, though piles can still be seen on the sea bed. And there was to be no replacement pier.

Last but by no means least, Tenby Royal Victoria, a short structure consisting of steel arches joining a seaward end landing stage, was demolished between 1946 and 1953.

Even those piers which survived this miserable time had not been immune to the wartime neglect, with Cleethorpes and Redcar already referred to as becoming shadows of their former selves. The work necessary throughout the country to rejoin the isolated parts sectioned in wartime was not done immediately, and few structures seem to have opened their doors to welcome paying customers the day or month after peace had been declared. Hastings, for instance, was not ready to take visitors until 1946, whilst Great Yarmouth Britannia remained closed for a further 12 months and needed repairs prior to reopening.

Lowestoft Claremont was another which required work, after looking abandoned and derelict by 1948; actor George Studd eventually took it over for a year and a reinforced concrete platform and new pavilion were built within the next two years. Felixstowe on the other hand suffered the same fate as Cleethorpes, with its isolated seaward end demolished when the war was over. Thankfully, at least the rest of the structure reopened.

Yet it would be entirely wrong to portray the immediate postwar years as being an era of unrivalled doom and gloom. For in many cases, the slow return to something approaching normality did in fact bring what might be called the 'last hurrah' before overall fortunes started to take a noticeable turn for the worse.

The phenomenon was not by any means limited to seaside piers. Professional football, to give an obvious example of mass culture, saw crowded stadiums week after week, whilst cricket's County Championship attained a popularity never to be reached again, helped no doubt by the glorious summer of 1947, and the run-scoring deeds of Messrs Compton and Edrich.

Southend Pier proves just how many were wanting to put their war troubles behind them and get on with enjoying their lives. Which the 'escapees' from London's East End did, putting a strain on the pier railway, reopened since VE Day, in the process. From the 1925 peak of just under two million, the number of passengers carried rose to 2,750,000 in 1946, and 3,300,000 a year later. A decision was therefore taken to purchase four completely new train 'sets', consisting of seven coaches in each, and costing £112,000 in all. The official maiden trip was made in April 1949, and the first full year of the line's operation saw it carry over 4,700,000 people; in addition, a further one million went through the ordinary turnstiles. This is believed to be a record for any pier: certainly its 'glory days' were back with a vengeance.

The pier railway at Southport also underwent changes, but for different reasons. Production of direct-current electricity supply ceased in the town (1950), necessitating either a conversion to alternating current or going over to diesel traction. It was decided on the latter option, and the line was regauged from 3ft 6in to 1ft 11½in. This began operating that May, using a steam-outline engine, itself replaced three years later.

Walton's pier railway had been of the same gauge as Southport's, but the old battery-run car had been damaged by a wartime fire, along with the pier and line itself. A 2ft-gauge contractor's line was however laid as a replacement, and this carried passengers after the pier reopened in 1948. Again, a steam-outline diesel engine provided the motive power – another artificial throwback to what it seemed nostalgia-seeking visitors wanted!

Southsea Clarence's extensive rebuilding has briefly been touched on. This was though no mere 'touching up', but a wholesale redevelopment. The first pile of the

Ryde from the Pier, I.W.

reconstructed lower pier was driven in 1953, with work on the superstructure commencing later at an estimated quarter of a million pounds. On 1 June 1961 the new Clarence Pier opened to the public, exactly 100 years after the original structure. Facilities included a 60ft-high observation tower, on what today is billed as being 'the largest amusement complex on the South Coast'. Unusually, the pier is wider than its length.

In South Wales, Mumbles Pier saw extensive reconstructing during the 1950s. Around 2,000 residents and well-wishers gathered at the pier-head as the Mayor of nearby Swansea performed the official reopening ceremony in June 1956. The VIP party then boarded the PS *Bristol Queen*, to inaugurate a regular pleasure steamer service, the first to operate from the pier for 17 years. Other attractions on that special day included a bathing beauty contest, dancing, yacht and rowing races, along with the launch of Mumbles lifeboat, based on the landing jetty.

As for the bomb-hit Lowestoft South, pier ownership

39784. MORECAMBE: ON THE SANDS AT HIGH TIDE.

had passed to the British Transport Dock Board on port nationalisation. The board leased the structure to the local council (later Waveney Borough Council), with some facilities franchised out by them at various times. On 2 March 1956, Prince Philip opened a new pavilion to replace the older reading room and entertainment pavilion.

Still in East Anglia, Great Yarmouth Britannia fell victim to yet another fire in April 1954. This destroyed the pier's third pavilion and the Ocean Ballroom. But though the latter wasn't replaced, the pier gained a new pavilion, opened in June 1958. This showed just how significant the pier was to a resort's entertainment values.

Developments at Ventnor were even more elaborate. The pier having been largely condemned after a 1948 survey, the local council sent a deputation to Whitehall to see what public help they could get. Their efforts were rewarded when it was agreed that 90% of the general maintenance costs, amounting to £76,000, would be awarded. No help, however, was given towards the £15,000 needed for a landing stage and entrance buildings.

RAMSEY, QUEEN'S – One of only two piers built on the Isle of Man, and the sole one surviving, this 2,241ft-long structure formally closed in 1991. However, a local 'Friends' group is fighting for its retention, and there have been special reopening days. An annual sum of £40,000 is set aside for repairs. *Author's Collection*

RAMSEY, I. O. M.

RHOS-ON-SEA – This is a real curiosity, in that the pier was first erected at Douglas on the Isle of Man! But even that didn't save it from eventual demolition in 1954. *Author's Collection*

THE PIER, RHOS-ON-SEA

Designed by Basil Phelps, work began in 1950. And though the public were allowed limited access once the decking was reinstated, the official opening of what was called the 'New Victoria Pier' did not take place until May 1955, with a Gala evening and firework display forming part of the celebrations.

Meanwhile the truncated pier at Cleethorpes was involved in 1955 in the saga of what was intended to be an offshore entertainment showboat.

As local resident John Coulam recalls:

'It wasn't to be stationary, but anchored by a seven-mile limit in the Humber near Halle Fort. In the interim we had to dig – I was the banksman organising this – an area 100ft long, 30ft deep and 15ft wide at the side of the breakwater near the pier. Thus when the tide came in, the ship could be pulled in here. Alas, the tug towing it had problems when it reached the pier, and steel ropes had to be placed round its pilings to shackle the vessel, originally bought from Sheerness, Kent, as a

EVERSFIELD PLACE, ST. LEONARDS - ON - SEA. No. X 5.

▲ ST LEONARDS, PALACE – This was an unlucky pier; it enjoyed success before ultimately becoming a casualty in 1951. It is seen here in the early 1920s, before an entrance was remodelled in Art Deco style. *Author's Collection*

◄ ST LEONARDS, PALACE – The 'Electric Theatre' seated 600-700 and was designed by F. H. Humphries. What with a seaward end skating rink (replacing a gale-damaged landing stage), the pier had much to offer! *Richard Riding Collection*

On the South Parade Pier.

business proposition. The excavator managed to pull it several yards, and we used wooden railway sleepers to help it reach the breakwater site.

'The people walked on the pier to see the stranded ship, and the Chairman of Cleethorpes Council – to whom the pier belonged – served the owners a summons after three months to have the boat removed. Not surprisingly one of them had a nervous breakdown, and went into a nursing home for several weeks.'

Such was the sad end of a bold experiment to keep up with the demand for new forms of leisure entertainment.

It was, however, at Deal where the most significant pre-1960 development took place. For at this Kentish resort a completely new pier was constructed to replace that destroyed during World War 2. The designers were Sir William Halcrow & Partners, with the Borough Engineer (the pier is council owned) responsible for the pier buildings. Costing £250,000, the main gangway consisted of 18 x 50ft spans supported by steel piles encased in concrete. At the seaward end was a three-deck pier-head, set at right angles to the approach and parallel to the promenade. Altogether the new Deal Pier measured 1,026ft by the time Prince Philip opened it in November 1957.

After Deal there were to be no more new British piers of the seaside variety – structures in Scotland at Scalasaig (1965) and Coll (1967) do not deserve to be regarded as such, and the same goes for the constructions on Lake Coniston (1980s), along with Weston-super-Mare's Sea Life Pier (1995).

But for a time, those remaining English and Welsh piers, all 67 of them, continued to attract their fair share of visitors. Maybe it was too late to claim that piers were still enjoying a golden age, yet having survived the war and its aftermath, the future, at least initially, seemed relatively bright. Sadly, however, things were quickly to change.

MUMBLES – An early 1900s view showing the pier, always popular with steamers, which opened the previous decade.
Author's Collection

21520 Mumbles Pier and Lighthouse Near Swansea

MUMBLES – Since 1937 the pier has been run by the Amusement Equipment Company, AMECO for short. Steamers still called, and additional facilities included a lifeboat station at the end of a landing jetty.
Richard Riding Collection

Brittannia Pavilion   Yarmouth

◄ **GREAT YARMOUTH, BRITANNIA** – The first Britannia Pier dated from 1858, and was replaced by the present structure which opened in 1901. Its pavilions have suffered badly from fire – this view shows the one which opened in 1902 and was destroyed in a blaze seven years later.
Richard Riding Collection

BRITANNIA PIER, GT. YARMOUTH. (31)

◄ **GREAT YARMOUTH, BRITANNIA** – The third pavilion can be seen in this pre-World War 2 view. It lasted from 1914-54, being replaced by the structure that still stands today.
Richard Riding Collection

VENTNOR, ROYAL VICTORIA – This is one of the saddest pier stories of recent years. The 'New Royal Victoria Pier' actually opened after rebuilding in 1955, but a massive £750,000 was needed for repairs by 1981. It seemed at one stage as if Ventnor Town Trust would succeed in raising the money needed (almost £250,000 was promised by South Wight Council), but it was not to be, and demolition took place in 1992/93. This view shows the pier between the wars.
Author's Collection

335. VENTNOR FROM THE WEST. – JUDGES'

VENTNOR, ROYAL VICTORIA – Another interwar view, showing the pier at its best. It actually replaced an earlier 1873 structure when it opened in 1887; the pavilion was added in 1906.
National Piers Society

843. "AFTER THE STORM." VENTNOR. I.O.W.   JUDGES'

POSTSCRIPT: THE YEARS OF DECLINE

Garth and Pier, Bangor

BANGOR, GARTH –
Opened in 1896, this plain
pier was the finest ever
built in Wales. It is seen
here in the Edwardian era,
when it was a popular
landing point for steamers.
Author's Collection

BANGOR, GARTH – The
pier has altered little over
the years, though it was
closed at the end of 1971 on
safety grounds. Thanks to
efforts of campaigners, led
by the City Council, the
restored pier opened its
gates again in 1988. This
view was taken in 1997
from the pier-head.
Author's Collection

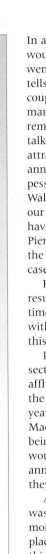

In a book such as this dedicated to its Golden Age, it would clearly be a mistake to dwell too much on what went wrong for the seaside pier. Indeed, my introduction tells us how fortunes have certainly improved over the last couple of decades. On top of this, there are the piers which managed to outride any social and economic storm, remaining arguably as popular as they had ever been. I am talking of the three Blackpool piers and their myriad new attractions, Brighton Palace and its more than two million annual visitors – the list is by no means as short as some pessimists might conceivably think. A survey by David Walker for the magazine *Portico* in 1978 claimed that '23 of our 45 fully open piers are economically viable, and should have a good future'. The first Chairman of the National Piers Society, John Hodgkins, was therefore right to decry the undue public attention on what he termed 'disaster cases'.

However, I believe that to understand their present resurgence, it is necessary to look briefly at why piers for a time began to be regarded as relics of a 'golden age'. As with the causes of their growth in the previous century, this involves factors of importance to the social historian.

Ironically for something firmly in the entertainment sector, piers were to lose out because of the increased affluence enjoyed by a majority of the British population – the reverse of what had happened nigh on a hundred years previously. For the fatter wage packets of Macmillan's 'you've never had it so good' nation were being used to take holidaymakers further afield. No longer would individuals be automatically content with their annual week or weeks at the English or Welsh seaside, they were wanting to travel abroad.

And it was no mere coincidence that foreign travel wasn't now just the preserve of the rich with the time and money to spare. Aeroplanes took the British traveller to places on the Continent, and package holidays made things not so much more expensive for them than if they had stayed at home. There were also the coach companies which organised breaks that incorporated boat journeys across the Channel, from ports such as Dover, just 22 miles from Calais.

And on the French Riviera or the Costa Brava, there was one big advantage for the holidaymaker – lots of sun! Deckchairs on a windswept seaside pier were deemed to be no match for sunbathing on an exotic beach.

The very newness of overseas destinations definitely appealed to a generation brought up in austerity Britain. What's more, they were more likely to be car owners, able to travel freely from place to place, moving on after an hour or two if a particular destination wasn't to their liking. This hadn't really been an option before, even when charabanc trips had increased people's mobility. For with any organised outing, you were still limited by the driver's choice and the wishes of the travelling majority. If, however, you had a car, then the world was your proverbial oyster. Individualism thus crept in more than ever before so far as holidays were concerned – why hang around on a railway station when you could simply drive?

Sadly, the British Tourist Industry wasn't so developed to fight back as it later became. Horror stories of the boarding house landladies throwing out guests from breakfast until supper time were hardly going to encourage people to remain loyal to their traditional holiday pattern. And the postwar boom had perhaps lulled some piers into a false sense of security – the same argument can be used with regard to British industry, and the lack of investment while profits continued to be recorded at respectful levels.

So as the 1970s approached, it really did seem that the 'glory days' of the seaside pier had gone for good. Thus we owe an awful lot to those who've done so much to ensure today's brighter outlook – men like John Lloyd and Brian Spielman at Brighton West, Peter Mason and the Elton family at Clevedon, George Gibbs at Bangor, and Don Hiett at Swanage. That's not forgetting the private owners who continued to have faith, including Anthony Brenner at Teignmouth who chaired 1996's 'Year of the Pier' campaign. Thanks to all of them, the optimism recorded in the introductory chapter is not misplaced. Piers can still, after all, have their Glory Days.

Swanage. from the Pier.

SWANAGE – There have actually been two piers at Swanage, and even today a few of the piles from the older 1859 structure are still visible. The current pier dates from 1896, and this view of promenaders dates from its first decade.
John Haddaway Collection

SWANAGE – The last steamer called in 1966, and after this, the pier began to fall into disrepair. It eventually ended up in the hands of the official receivers, who handed over control to Swanage Pier Trust in 1994. A grand reopening took place in the summer of 1998.
Richard Riding Collection

INDEX OF LOCATIONS ILLUSTRATED